"Mr. Gish, may I go to the bathroom?"

MY FIRST YEAR AS A HIGH SCHOOL TEACHER

Steven C. Gish

PEANUT BUTTER
PUBLISHING

Seattle, Washington

Printed in the United States of America

11.0084

ISBN 0-89716-520-9

Library of Congress Catalog Card Number:
94-066786

Cover Design:
David Marty Design

Editor:
Martha McDonough

Published by:

Peanut Butter Publishing
226 Second Avenue West
Seattle, Washington 98119
(206) 281-5965

About the Author

Steve Gish is a Social Studies teacher at Port Angeles High School in Port Angeles, Washington. Before becoming a teacher, he was a lawyer for about fourteen years. He lives with his wife and five kids on an unfinished mini-farm outside of town, where among other things, he tries to do the laundry.

Dedication

While this is the first thing you will read in this book, it is the last thing I am writing, almost literally on the eve of sending the manuscript off to the publisher.

As I look back over this adventure, I could focus on either the smaller or bigger picture. By smaller, I don't mean less, just more recent and apparent — like the tip of the iceberg. In that category I dedicate this work to the students who try, who make a meaningful job also fun. And also to those interested in schools, either as concerned citizens, or as those interested in teaching as a profession.

For every tip, there is a foundation. Without the support, help and patience of my wife and kids, who came with me as we planted our feet firmly in mid-air, I never would have had the chance to try.

Thank you.

Introduction

The following is a list of Who's Who in education in America today: The PTA, the School Board, the School Superintendent, the Principal, Parents, Students, Psychologists, Counselors, Education Professors and probably many others. That's also a list of who this book is not about. This book is about the teacher. It is one rookie's personal, daily experiences dealing with the everyday issues a new teacher faces. Or dodges.

It is June, and I just finished my first year as a teacher. Last fall, just before school started, I began a daily journal about this year. This book is a walk through my journal. As my legal ethics professor once said, as we go on this walk I suggest you don't wear your nice shoes. If it goes right, this book should at times be embarrassing — a little for me and a little for our educational system. If it's not, that means I wasn't honest enough, because neither I nor the system are good enough to not be embarrassed by some of what happened.

As with many first attempts, I wish I could do it over again, but I'm glad I don't have to. I'd like to do it over because my students deserved better. But I realize that no teacher is perfect so I'm glad to have my first year of fumbling and insecurity behind me. Now I can go on to my second year of fumbling and insecurity.

As word got out that I was writing this, everyone said, "Steve, make it funny. That's the only way it'll be appealing or go anywhere." My response to that is that this work is not meant to be entertaining so much as it is to be informative. However, without even trying, a report on the life of a first-year teacher is both. Possibly, the value of the book is that it has not been doctored for entertainment's sake.

If you are curious about what really happens in the mind of a rookie teacher trying to make it, and what really happens in the classroom, this book will give you a year-long glimpse inside that closed door in the 400 hall. If you have no high school teaching experience and you are either curious or, if you are a prospective teacher, anxious about the whole thing, you are where I was nine months ago. Not that I don't have anxiety now, getting ready for next year, but facing the unknown of the first year is unique. Thankfully.

This Introduction and the last chapter, "A Look Back — And Ahead," are the only portions of the book created after the year was over. The journal was written as it happened. Generally I would write about one page per evening, re-living the events of the day with some reactions and anticipations thrown in. Occasionally I later added an observation or note to emphasize or clarify a point, problem or opportunity. Other than that, I am telling the events as expressed in the journal. It is a better witness to the year than I can now be. It was written on the spot, from the perspective of an anxious rookie, a viewpoint that I think cannot be recreated once the year is over and the experience of the first year is behind you. Had I waited, or written from the perspective of having completed the year, I no longer would've been able to see the trees — I would be one of them.

This book is divided into weeks. Some weeks are divided by which day I made a certain entry. Some weeks skip some days. Some are not divided like that at all. They are a more general recollection of the events and reactions in a certain week. I was tempted to include a "Topics For Discussion" section at the end of each week, but I decided against that because I realized that as you read, certain issues, questions and miscellaneous opportunities for discussion and argument about my myriad of shortcomings come screaming out at you. You don't need to be led, or more probably limited, by topics that I suggest are ripe for further discussion or thought. You'll see plenty.

You will see the unrelenting schedule a teacher faces, preparing for five classes per day. It is like a treadmill powered by gravity. It just doesn't stop.

I haven't reported everything that happened everyday. In my defense, if one is necessary or possible, the days or moments I left out generally were when things went well, or at least went according to plan and were uneventful. I think there were days like that. I have tried to include any unusual success, because they certainly are part of the year. But, just like the TV news, you don't report that today there was no accident at the corner of 3rd and Park.

There are times where someone said or did something that deserved to be in here, and therefore has been included, even though it may not seem to be related to a topic I'm dealing with. I would rather report the event crudely than leave it out because it didn't look like it flowed well with the writing. At school, often, maybe always, a day or even an hour doesn't flow real well, either.

I deal very little with the content of what I taught. You won't find much about detailed lesson plans, or specific subject information. There are plenty of books about those things by people who are actually qualified to write about them. I'm reminded of the saying about a basketball team having a good game plan, and on paper they look unbeatable. But as someone has pointed out, the game isn't played on paper. I think that realization to some degree also applies to lesson plans and the classroom.

There are major issues in education today dealing with revolutionizing the entire process, including curriculum, scheduling and expectations. This book is not meant to be about any of that high-level stuff. It is not a scholarly work, in the same way that the play-by-play of an NBA game is not scholarly. However, in the latter part of the year I find myself making comments about the failings of our education system and offering some suggestions about how to improve things.

In many things you read it seems like you need to go through a lot of words to sift out a few gems. This won't be any different, except there may be no gems, but the many words could have a value of their own. The routine is a core part of the experience, and you will see some, perhaps much, repetition. It is part of our educational system. If you can't handle repetition you won't like our education system today.

While this book is not intended to be about my personal life, to get a better understanding of this book and my perspective, you should know something about me and why I became a teacher.

About three years ago I reached a crossroad. I had been a lawyer for 13 years and had grown tired of the adversity and stress that you wear in that career, and was tired of putting Band-Aids on cancer. At that time my wife and I had three small children, one mortgage and those other daily responsibilities that pile up on us all. Engineering a career change wasn't practical, but I was really looking for a change.

I wanted to do something that would put me in a position where my actions would have a positive, meaningful affect on many people — and be totally fun. But I was flexible and realistic, so I figured I'd better look for something that could be fairly meaningful and which might be somewhat fun. I decided to become a high school teacher.

In law, the likelihood is that if there is a winner, there is a loser. I'd been both many times, and even the wins began to lose their thrill. In education, I guessed, if there is a winner there are several winners. A nice change. I would see.

Anyway, after I closed my law office, I worked part time as Judge Pro Tem, much of the time in Juvenile and Divorce courts. That on-call work relieved me of any ongoing client obligations, provided sufficient income to cover the transition period, and prepared us to live on a teacher's salary. My judging experience also provided a valuable perspective on teen and family issues, which certainly are a factor in the public schools.

I did all the stuff I needed to do to get my teaching certificate, and applied at many places for a job. To my total amazement, I was rejected at schools I had applied to. I thought, given my background, I'd be a shoe-in wherever I applied. Nope. So I taught — no, served — as a substitute teacher for a little over a year. Then a teaching job opened up at a high school in a small community which my wife and I thought would be a great place to move to. I applied for — no, I courted — that job, and got hired. I would teach Social Studies at a large (1,500) high school in a small (17,000) town in western Washington state. Also, I would be coaching a little. I would be sweating a lot.

We moved to this area only a few days before my school duties were to start. We bought a house not yet completed. The person who built the house did not want to pay the cost of running power into the property. The house is in the woods, about a quarter mile away from the main road and about 15 to 20 minutes from school. In other words, I moved my wife and four small sons to a remote area where we don't know anyone into a house without power so I could do a job I had never done before. Works for me.

Someone said it would be important for me to mention that my wife and I homeschool our first and third graders. My wife does over 99 percent of that teaching. This book is not an analysis of the various kinds of schooling available, though a few times in the book I do make some comparisons between public and homeschooling. It is helpful to have that perspective, but this is about my first year as a public school teacher, and the few times I do make comments or comparisons are from the viewpoint of a rookie high school teacher hoping to make public school better.

I am writing this book about my experience for several reasons. One is that I would like to help people interested in education as a career get a first-hand picture of the real world in school from someone who is only one step ahead of them. That was lacking in my training, and hopefully a book like this will be of use to a few future teachers, or possibly even more importantly, to a few who may learn ahead of time that they don't want to teach. I am aware of people who abandon careers and take out second mortgages to go back to school to get a teaching certificate. Unfortunately, only *after* being in the classroom do they realize it isn't for them.

What qualifications do I have to write this? I catch myself wondering how my colleagues down the hall, or for that matter any veteran teacher who reads this, will react. "Why is he writing a book about teaching? It was only his first year."

My response is that this is necessarily not a "How To" book. In fact, many times it becomes a "How Not To" book. I make no claims that I was a great, good or even at times adequate teacher. But I learned. This is written so the reader can learn from my year.

As I recall the year and go through my journal, I sometimes cringe at what I said or did. Or didn't say or do. A lot happens in the course of a year, and it's not going to be perfect. I make statements or have ideas in the beginning of the year which by the end of the year I realize were wrong. But they are in there so you can see the progression. Or digression-you decide. I especially cringe at the insecurity that I lived with during the year. I was constantly wondering how I was doing, and how I was being perceived by students, teachers and administrators. However, that may be excusable in the first year of a profession that has a high wash-out rate.

On the last day of school, I told my students about this journal. I had just received favorable news from a publisher, and we were all a bit excited about the whole thing. After all, they have leading roles here. But more than that, I believed them when they said they want to read this if it actually becomes a book. I write this knowing I will be facing them again in different classes or on the street, and they will know if I have told the story truthfully. They were there, everyday. They will be my conscience as I complete this and am tempted to leave out a bad part or somehow try to make myself look good.

Therefore, without regard to the embarrassments, mistakes and failures it reveals, this book will stay true to the journal. Any editing is done only to clean up bad or hurried grammar or to simply make the tale more readable. But never to make the tale, or the teller, appear better, more successful or interesting than the events reveal.

The Days Before Classes Start

Today we met with the school district leaders with titles no one can remember and who gave several welcome-to-school talks. One man said something that appealed to me. His point was that it is okay to make mistakes. I really think he was looking at me when he said that.

Thursday, September 3rd, five days before classes start. Today was my first scheduled day of work. It was "rookie day," when all the new teachers attend various orientation meetings. There are seven of us who are new to the high school, but only two actual rookie teachers. We stick out. We seem to be smiling more than others, probably out of a naive belief that this is fun. Mostly, we're nervous and don't know what else to do, and we're looking for all the help we can get. Tomorrow, all the teachers will be here. The first day of classes will be Tuesday, because Monday is Labor Day. I guess as of today, it's too late to turn back.

At an orientation meeting we were told, "Be innovative, and if you have a doubt about a new topic or approach, go ahead and try it." I got relief from that, knowing that a failed plan or idea here and there would be accepted as at least a good try. And now I had someone else to blame.

We received all sorts of papers regarding rules and where to go for this and that. I admit to not reading all of the stuff they gave us. It would've taken less time to read *War and Peace*. Also, there were issues that came up now that I am a state employee. For example, many of us had several questions about health care. I didn't want to be bothered with that, but it was a necessary part of orientation. I stuffed it all in a file and figured I'd read it later. Right.

Even though today was the first official day, I've been in and out of my classroom for a couple days getting ready, I thought, for the year. Actually, I wasn't doing anything productive, because I was both a bit too excited to sit down and do real preparation, and so much a rookie that I don't know what preparation is necessary.

I am taking over the room used by a veteran who has moved on, and there is a lot of stuff in there, none of which I feel I have the authority to do much with. An exception to that is the walls. I took down what

I considered to be outdated materials and started fresh. My goal is to have more or less a current events wall, with places for opinions from the Right and Left, other news, quotes, a comedy section and a section for student contributions. I made space for those. I could get headings made for those sections later, maybe by the students. I found two useable wall maps, one of the world and one of the United States. Up they went. Beyond that, there are boxes and boxes of old stuff around, and I don't feel comfortable removing anything until I see how that is handled. And I have no idea what will or won't be useful.

I made about a half page of class rules. They are very mild. I think that if you treat people with respect, they'll act accordingly. I don't want to be seen as a new guy coming in with dozens of rules, get perceived as being strict, and lose the chance to have a good rapport with the kids before we even get started.

Today the principal, who is very helpful and non-threatening, cornered me to talk about an incident that came up. One of the veteran teachers was just accused of some sort of sexual inappropriateness with one or more current or former students, and he would be suspended pending an investigation. This news was about to come out in the newspaper, and the principal wanted to tell us before we read about it.

The issue of whether, when or how to ever have any physical contact with a student is, well, touchy. And I mean any contact, not just something that is obviously wrong. I'm talking about even a pat on the shoulder, a handshake or a high-five. I think it will be smart to have no contact whatsoever.

Friday, September 4th. All teachers were on campus for a welcome-back faculty meeting. A few teachers had heard there was a lawyer coming on board, and after the meeting, came up and wanted to know why a lawyer would want to become a teacher. I tried to tell them, but I noticed I never sounded too convincing. Maybe I'm not cut out for this after all. Those with lawyer-friends said no explanation was necessary. I met other teachers in the Social Studies department, and they were all very helpful. After the all-teachers meeting, most teachers disappeared, I presumed, to their rooms to make last-minute preparations for the first day of school. Perhaps many of them simply left, or went to a place to socialize that I don't know about. I don't know what it takes for a veteran to prepare, but the campus seemed pretty quiet. I was in my room trying to be productive. I have a great deal of respect for good teachers, because there are character traits you can't quite describe, but which you can see in action. In my case, the only character traits I am able to muster are nervous apprehension, randomness and ignorance. I didn't know what to do, but I was doing it very quickly.

In the evening, our principal had an open house for the new teachers. We milled around, ate and talked. It was a bit empty for me, because no matter how nice the evening was, it was still getting closer to Tuesday morning, when the bell would ring and I'd be flying solo in front of the class. No amount of comfortable chit-chat would reduce the anxiety surrounding the whole reason we were there.

Monday, September 7th. It is the night before school starts. This evening I went into the neighboring classroom where a 34-year veteran teaches. He had everything on his desk laid out perfectly, with a written plan for each phase of each period of the day, as if a substitute could come in and teach the class. I determined right then — that would be my goal, to have my room and desk ready like that each day.

I went back to my room and something wasn't right. It was the room. I rearranged my desk and work area into the same arrangement used by the veteran. There, it looked right, and was a better use of the space. Unlike the veteran, who has his desks in rows, I arranged the class in a "U" shape, with only a first and second row. My goal is to have a "seminar" feel to my classes, to promote discussion. I don't want anyone to feel left out, and if the physical arrangement can facilitate that, good. The podium and overhead projector are in front, at the opening of the "U," but I hope to walk around in the middle or back of the room during the discussions.

Now I was on track. I had a notebook divided into three sections for the three different subjects I'd teach. Even though I had three sections of History/Government, I would just have one section for it and repeat it during the day as necessary. I'd have a plan for each class, and simply have a new piece of paper for each day. Voila. I would invent the wheel this year, and have it organized for next. And, using the three-ring notebook method, I could slip in new material as it came up. I had a plan, and felt relieved. It was finally hitting me about how much preparation I had not done prior to this, now about 12 hours away from the first class. The reason I didn't have something like that going two months earlier can be partially explained by my schedule in the summer which I mentioned earlier.

Tomorrow is the first day. I remember all I'd been through to get to this moment. Leaving a career behind to take what most people would say is a step backwards; working part time while commuting a couple hours, several times a week for about a year to earn my teaching certificate; applying to many places and not even getting an interview, and finally landing a job in what we consider a great location.

I have my clothes set out. "A little better than the kids," is how the principal described his hopes for how teachers would dress, though there were no set rules. My rule would be to dress so that no one will notice when I pit out. Anyway, the alarm is set, though it won't be necessary.

Unless I run away in the middle of the night, it is about to start.

✒ 1st Week: Sept. 8th - 11th

The roll was done. I walked to the middle of the room and asked for their attention. They actually quieted down ...This was THE moment.

September 8th. It is the evening after the first day. When I arrived at school this morning, I felt totally unprepared. We were told that for the first two days or more, don't issue books. Kids are feeling out their schedules and will try to change them on such basis as they don't want to be in a class with an old girlfriend. They also will try to use frivolous reasons. Though the counselors don't allow changes without a good cause, students will be coming and going for a few days. The classes you see on the first day aren't necessarily the ones you'll see the second or third days.

In the meantime, I had to invent something that would be appropriate for each of my classes. I had prepared handouts for a lesson on Bloom's Taxonomy (a hierarchy of what we do with new facts we acquire, from basic memorization to sophisticated evaluation), my class rules, and a lesson I devised yesterday in which the students define educational terms such as teaching, learning, school and success. I had them define a good student. I will be able to have them refer to their own definitions later in case any confusion develops.

I also gave them an assignment regarding liberal and conservative labels used in politics and in the media. I got that one this morning about a half-hour before school started. A sympathetic teacher felt I might need some material to start with. He was right. I hustled over to the copy center in a back room of the library figuring I'd whip out a quick 150 copies to make sure I had enough material to cover the first day. When I got to the copy room, I discovered that apparently I wasn't the only one facing the time crunch. The line-up was long, but I was desperate so I hung around, tried not to act nervous, and got the job done. Am I going to be scraping around like this every day?

My schedule is: 1st period, U.S. History and Government; 2nd period, Math For Daily Living; 3rd, another U.S. History and Government; 4th period planning; a half hour for lunch; 5th period Teen Law and Current Events; and 6th period, another U.S. History and Government. That amounts to three "preps." The day starts at 7:45 and ends at 2:30.

7:45. The first class. They walked in and, remarkably, actually sat in their seats and didn't simply blow me up or light the room on fire.

I allowed the kids to sit wherever they wanted. I would deal with a seating chart in a few days. Taking roll was a bit of a chore, having to call out about 30 names and not knowing if the people responding are who they say they are. A necessary evil, I guess. During orientation, the principal only half-jokingly wished there was a method of taking roll by having something like a scanner simply note who passed through the door. After one day I think I fully appreciate what he was saying.

The roll was done. I walked to the middle of the room and asked for their attention. They actually quieted down, like in that awkward moment when you are in a noisy room and you lean over to tell something to someone, and just as you begin to talk the entire room quiets down and stares at you. Anyway, I had their attention. Now what? This was THE moment. If I didn't know it before, I learned right away that one component of being a successful teacher is to be a good extemporaneous speaker.

I introduced myself and invited them to ask questions about me. I pointed out that, like it or not, I was about to become a significant, or at least a constant, factor in their lives. What would they like to know about me? We discussed my law career, and why I made the change. That got interest aroused and gave us something to break the ice. After that topic ran it's course, I moved on to a discussion of my handouts. I wanted to get them thinking in terms of what is going to be happening during the learning process, and create some interest and questions which they may not have thought about before. Fortunately, it all came out fairly easily, and we were off.

Class conduct first period was typical of the three history classes, and was better than I expected. In my education classes there was much concern, though few answers, regarding how to handle discipline problems. I think because of my law career I've been trained to expect the worst and have a response ready. I need to learn that school is not an adversary setting, and that we are here to work for each other. That is a wonderful change in my life which I will not be able to comprehend and integrate into my personality overnight.

At the beginning of my 2nd period math class, there is a 15-minute program that is shown on TVs provided in each room. It comes on automatically, creating a little bit of a "Big Brother" feeling. It's called *Channel One*, and it's a national news program, put on for students in

11

middle and high schools across the country. It's as if you were watching any network news show, except the reporters and anchors are in their late teens, and the show bends over backwards to appeal to students by always being "hip." (I don't think it's cool to say cool, but I'm learning.) For instance, rock or rap music (is "rap music" an oxymoron?) are used regularly to phase in and out of the breaks. The content and presentations seem useful. However, *Channel One* also runs commercials. I've been told it's a hot issue locally because some in town are adamantly opposed to having commercials in the schools. I'll watch and figure out my opinion as time goes on.

I'm teaching a basic math class because, as near as I can figure out, they need two periods of this basic math class covered, and there were two vacant periods in the Social Studies department waiting for a spot. Voila. They tabbed a veteran and me to each cover one of the math periods. I'm not a math major. Or minor. I told my class this, and that through the year we can learn the material together.

I'm glad for the chance to teach a basic math class. It's not really math, it's motivation. I look forward to trying it as an interesting contrast to my other classes.

3rd period History went just like 1st, though it is a smaller class. When I was done with 3rd period and had my planning period and lunch ahead, I experienced an amazing amount of relief, as though a pressure valve were released. I got out of my room, pretending to be going on an errand to the office or library. My real purpose was just to get out, get a pop and exchange some high-fives with other teachers who had also made it through such an intense morning. Kind of a camaraderie which develops when people go through a shared experience. Also, I was a bit proud that I was now a teacher, and I enjoyed getting recognized as such. I felt and acted like a kid. Totally silly and self-centered. Totally true.

For lunch, I brown-bagged it in the faculty lunch area in the back of the kitchen. For the most part I kept my mouth shut and my ears open. I've had a few friends get out of teaching, not because of the kids, but because of the cynical or immature attitude some teachers have regarding their profession. I don't sense any problems in that regard with anything I've seen so far.

The day progressed fine. Fifth and sixth periods went like the morning classes. I didn't know how I would react to teaching the same thing three periods a day. Actually, today all five were pretty much the same. But it was all so new that a feeling of boredom or repetition never entered my mind. I'll leave the feeling of boredom to the students, where it belongs.

When the day ended, I was relieved. Maybe I can do this, and maybe I'll even enjoy it. About a year ago, one of my former high school teachers told me that if I find myself not enjoying teaching, get out. Don't inflict the kids or yourself with your anger or discontent. I'd remembered that, and was waiting to see my reaction. So far so good. I at least would make it all the way to my second day.

As I get ready for tomorrow, I find that I'm scraping for things to do until I can get into the texts. I stumbled onto what looks like a useful planning method. I have started using the three-ring binder. For each period, I simply have a page for each date in the immediate future, and will write what I intend to do that period on that date. This gives me more space than a simple lesson plan book, so I can write down anecdotes I want to throw in, or after a class put in interesting twists which came up, and have the hour more fully "scripted" if I want to. The three-ring notebook is good because if there is a handout for that day, I can insert it, or other material, so next time through that class I have the whole plan with handouts ready to go. It would be very good help for a substitute, also.

Wednesday. The only real assignment I gave yesterday was to answer questions regarding education and the process generally. We then discussed them today. This is filler stuff, though helpful and valid, until we get our final class lists and can issue texts.

In the teachers' eating area behind the kitchen, there is constantly a tray of goodies of some sort. I hustled over there between 2nd and 3rd periods to get a treat. I think that will become a habit. My second period math class is a challenge, and it's a bit of a relief when it's over. Cookie time.

It seems that many rules will get created or defined by the necessity of the moment. For some reason, I now have the rule that only one person of each sex can go the bathroom at a time. I didn't think of that ahead of time and it's not written anywhere that I know about, but it just sort of happened.

Thursday. I issued books today. In most classes that, combined with introductions to the book, took up the 55 minutes. I'd been warned to be very careful to make sure that I got all the serial numbers and names correct because at the end of the year I'd need an exact accounting. The history text, about six years old, is your basic history book. My plan is to go chronologically through it.

I can see that I have a lot of reading to do. I will literally be staying just ahead of my students. One problem is that I have just an adequate knowledge of U.S. history. With my background in law, I could come up with interesting assignments and projects, but for the guts of the history course I will for the most part just be staying ahead of the kids in the book. In my student teaching I taught History using a different text, and admitted I would be going through this book for the first time with them. That honest admission hopefully will alleviate some stress, but doesn't relieve me of my duty to be their teacher, and have something to offer. I can see that will be a source of pressure all year.

I intend to go through the book by having each student give an oral report on a given section of whatever chapter we are in. That way, they'll be accountable to the class for their section, and will learn in the fullest way — by teaching. Each student will take notes on what the other students are teaching. I'll be at the overhead, steering and repeating. They will be given points if they outline their assigned section and do their oral report.

In Math, I will assign the lesson and go over it in class. My goal is not to hide the ball, but to help the students learn. I suspect they'll get all 10s on the daily work, mostly because I'll be giving the processes and answers. The kids got mad at me when I told them I was thinking of not giving them credit for their homework and just grading them on their tests. I did what looked like a quick about-face, though the substance of what would really count on their grade didn't really change. I've decided to give them some credit for their homework, but the bulk of their grade will be on the tests. That could sound like a lot of daily correcting to do but for the obvious answer: "Pass your paper two people to the left." They correct each other's. Voila. As long as the answer key works, I'm a genius. The tests will serve as measurements for purposes of grading.

My 5th period law class is wild. They are very animated, and it doesn't help much that this class is right after lunch. It will be a test of my patience, and that's a muscle that needs testing anyway. I'm in the right place for that. I handed out the Street Law books and we were off. Also, it is election time, and I arranged for one of the candidates for a Judge position to speak to the class. He was fine and the hour went well, partly because I bribed the class with one point per question which they prepared ahead of time to ask our guest. Tomorrow I have his opponent coming in. The timing of the election is fortuitous and is making my law class easier for me and interesting for the kids. I feel proud that I was able to arrange live, relevant speakers during the first week.

My classes have been functioning about like I thought they would, though not as, well, exciting as they ought to be. In Law, for instance, I would bring up a topic from the book, and talk about the points with the kids. I am not having as much success as I thought regarding drawing the kids into the conversation. I envisioned having animated discussions in which the students would be so involved and excited that they would not want to leave class even after the bell went off. Some participate, but others seem to be envisioning their week-end.

Friday. Some teachers showed videos this week, and in hindsight I can see that this week would have been a good time to show one. But that brings up the subject of videos, and in the long run I don't want to be known as a teacher who has a "plan in the can." Several kids mentioned some classes show too many films and it gets boring. I am aware of and want to avoid the "Conspiracy of the Least" referred to by Theodore Sizer in *Horace's Compromise*. That is a scenario where the teacher demands the least of the students he can, they live down to his expectations, no one does much work and everyone is happy.

A main problem this week is that I did not prepare enough for each class. When the bell goes off, you are standing in front of 30 or so kids who are waiting for something brilliant to happen. And there I am. Brilliant probably won't happen even if you have it planned, and certainly won't happen if you don't. Having a class go well is largely a function of how much time you spend preparing. With no power at my house, when we have lights out, it's really lights out. Running on a generator for an hour or two after dinner to get the four kids settled in bed is all we are doing. There is no time to stay up and do plans, etc. That's a good, but not real reason why I didn't do as much as I could. The real reason is that by 9:00 p.m. I am pooped, and all I could do is flop in bed. I didn't realize how much work it is.

Seating charts. In order to get to know my students by name it will help to get their names on a chart. In four of my classes I was able to accomplish this today. It really helped. In my fifth period class, as I write this Friday afternoon, I still have no idea of the names of 95

15

percent of the kids in there. Monday I will get that chart done, and have no more excuses.

The week has gone well. My colleagues are very helpful and willing to share some of their hand-out material and advice on whatever comes up. I am thinking of the things that could've gone wrong but didn't. No real gaffes, no conflicts with kids, no parent calls regarding something I've done. In short, no anarchy. So far so good. The possibility is here to teach.

As I typed this in the faculty lounge on Friday afternoon, I was interrupted by my name being blared over the campus-wide (it sounds like city-wide) loudspeaker: "MR. GISH, YOU'RE WANTED IN THE BUSINESS OFFICE. MR. GISH, YOU'RE WANTED IN THE BUSINESS OFFICE." That is startling the first time it happens, and conjures up all sorts of anxieties. As I hustled to the office to answer the page, I wondered if some of the unread fine print of my contract had a one-week out clause for the district, or about whom had I offended so that they wanted to talk to me about it on a Friday afternoon? It turns out it was a phone call from a fellow teacher asking if I wanted to play golf. What else can go right?

✏ 2nd Week: Sept. 14th - 18th

Someone asked if I'm enjoying myself or if there is a lot of pressure. The answer lies in one word: Preparation. Preparation is to teaching like location is to real estate. If it's not there, it's not a good deal. When you're about to face 30 kids with either no plan or a bad one, you feel the pressure and it's not enjoyable. I've already been there.

Monday night. The generator is on so I've got a few minutes at home to get down my thoughts.

Last Friday night I went to the first home football game of the season. I saw only one other teacher, and only for a second. There were probably a dozen or more there whom I don't recognize yet. If you haven't gone to a high school football game lately, it's a lot like going to the mall, except colder. Junior and senior high kids are checking out the action, occasionally taking a break to watch the game. The adults are trying to get the business at hand done, which is watch the game or their player/son and chat with friends.

Over the weekend, someone put glue in many of the locks around the school. Today one of my students wanted to go wash his hands, and came back asking how you get superglue off your hands. I suspected nothing, but the student told me a different teacher had seen him and sent him to the office accusing him of the glue incident. He was cleared as a "suspect," but I guess I've got to become more suspicious or more aware, or both.

I inadvertently said something the kids latched on to. In Teen Law we discussed having another set of guest speakers in, and the kids wanted to know if they had to have questions prepared like before. I told them not to think of it as an assignment but as an opportunity to be challenging, yet respectful. They actually reacted positively to that. Give a teen a chance to challenge an authority figure and you've got their attention.

Wednesday. Today in my law class things went well for all the wrong reasons. My goal was to have the students learn to distinguish between new legal terms. It was loosely planned to be a walk through a portion of the first chapter, with me lecturing, bringing up examples and answering questions. What really happened was that the Socratic method erupted, with me asking the students questions about basic law topics, attempting to draw out answers which would eventually lead to clarification and practical application of the topic at hand. They went with it, and the hour flew by. After the bell, I went to my plan book, which is evolving by accident, and wrote down an outline for what I had just done. That's not preparation, and it doesn't feel good. On the plus side, I guess that's also a function of being flexible. It would've been better had I actually prepared an outline before class, but it didn't happen. Maybe certain things can't be prepared ahead of time, and the seat-of-the-pants method has its (limited) place.

I'm teaching my history classes by dividing each chapter into several two-page sections and assigning each student to outline one section and orally report to the class. Some of the kids who haven't been prepared for their turn actually have come up after class and apologized for not being ready. That's different than the few who have come up and rationalized why they weren't ready, and asked for permission to turn it in late. Some of the apologizers are the types I would guess would not want their friends to know they actually talked to a teacher intentionally, let alone apologized for not being ready. I'm being easy in allowing people to turn stuff in late.

My math class potentially could take a lot of time. However, I've started the "pass your paper two to the left" routine for correction, and have pretty much trusted that the kids are actually marking a mistake as wrong when told to. With the scores I've seen, I feel safe in this assumption.

It is already clear that this math class is going to be a different, and perhaps untamed, animal. The assignments are like those of any topic — they're not hard unless you don't understand the stuff, and then they're impossible. My job will be to take those who are willing (and cause the rest to become willing) from apathy and fog to enthusiasm and clarity. I will be trying this with a group whose main interest is figuring out what they want for a snack.

I should point out that I have allowed food in class. Given that this math class is very independent (another way of saying out of control?) I don't mind allowing them to do this. During the hour, some kids are chatting, some are working on the assignment, some doing a combination of those, while I am milling about trying to help with the assignment, or working problems on the overhead projector. Everyone is to have the assignment done by the end of the hour. I think it's about like a math class is supposed to be, but I feel close to losing control. I suppose I'm too liberal when I allow the kids to leave the room — that loosens things up a bit too much. But nothing specific has happened to make me withdraw the privilege, so for now I won't.

There is another battle going on, and it's not just in Math — it's in all the classes. I'm trying to run them in such a way that I'm doing my job yet doing it in a way that the kids will like me. But I'm trying to resist falling into the trap of altering my personality and approach just to be friends with the kids. That would be the easy way out. The harder, better way is to be their teacher. The kind they will respect when they're old enough to look back with a more mature outlook. That's a hard thing to do. There is a fine line there, and I certainly don't have it figured out. When all the figuring out is done, it will probably have a lot to do with being yourself and treating everyone with respect.

I made my first history test today. For my tests, I am allowing the kids to use their notes. Not their books, just their notes. My reasons for this need some explanation.

My approach to teaching anything is to make it as applicable to real life as possible. I really don't like tests which require memorization of something which will get forgotten the next day. Also, the usual situation in life is that you get to use your notes. People are referring to manuals all the time. My better reasons are that I hope the students in my classes will become active participants, and the only way they can do that is by paying attention. A good motivator is to have the kids know that they can bring the answers into the test, if they have paid attention and taken notes. That should help create a focused classroom. Additionally, the one time you've really got the class's attention is during a test. Rather than have it be a defeating experience, why not have it be a learning experience? If I can have them take one more walk through their notes, take some of the facts out, think about them and apply them to a question, what's wrong with that? I asked a veteran about this, and he said he's tried it both ways. I took that as an okay, to see how it goes.

The test I created is a combination of matching and essay. A little something for everyone to argue about, I guess. I copied some of the past year's teacher's questions, and came up with some of my own. My goal is to use the higher Bloom's levels, and get away from rote memorization.

19

One of my classes is too rowdy. I learned today, though, that I can't blame the students for not paying attention unless what I have planned to offer in class is better than what they are chatting about with their neighbor. A veteran teacher said don't blame the students for your lack of preparation. I learned that today.

Friday. My math class may get humdrum real soon. Since today was Friday, and we'd just finished a test yesterday and have been doing an assignment a day for a week, I figured I'd give them a sort of day off. That is to say, they had an assignment, but I didn't make it due by the end of the period, which translates in the student's brain to, "I don't have to do this now, so I'll sit around and chat." After school, I went to the math department head to get ideas for fun and/or interesting math games and exercises. Something to break up the routine, but still be somewhere in the math realm. Moral of the story: Know who the resource people are for those types of things and ask for help if you need it.

I showed my first movie today. It fits in with the history material, and a veteran in the department just got through showing it, but I feel a bit guilty plopping the kids in front of a movie. I suppose a good litmus test of how you feel about what's going on in class is whether or not you'd like the principal to be popping in on what you're doing. Let's just say I'm glad the principal didn't pop in today.

During lunch, my room gets invaded by a group of students in a club against drunk driving. The club, as near as I can tell in the first couple weeks, has not discussed any issues related to drunk driving. It's more of a Dungeons and Dragons club, with a few medieval war buffs thrown in. On Thursday someone spilled pop, leaving a sticky mess. I closed the room to the club for three days. A little exercise of unilateral consequence setting. It was my first real discipline action since the year started, and I was wondering what would be the response. There was none. I'd heard that the previous teacher did about the same thing, only a bit harsher. I'll see if they keep the room cleaner from now on.

I corrected the tests in U.S. History today. I am amazed at what some of the kids missed. Of course, someone's reaction could be that I just didn't teach the material well. Given the things they missed, it is more clear that some kids just did not do any work or pay any attention. Questions like, "What was this chapter about?" are not rocket scientist questions. I asked that particular question to determine if some were paying as little attention as I suspected. Unfortunately, I was right. On the flip side, several students missed none or only one so I suppose there was an appropriate variety of scores, but I find myself thinking of those who did lousy. Obviously, I may have some who simply can't read or write well. I will be more aware of those students and deal with them and their counselor individually. I will go a bit slower and be a bit more basic. I will also teach a bit on study skills or listening skills that can be applied anywhere.

That approach opens me to the charge of "dumbing down" the class. I don't like to think of it in those terms because I will continue to feel out what pace I can use, and how the kids react. Even some of the students who got higher grades were urging me to go slower or repeat ideas. The search for the appropriate presentation speed and level is on.

Besides the history tests, the only homework I brought home for the weekend is my history notebook, in which I keep my running outline of the text. I've asked the students to do the same, and I better stay ahead of them. I'd like to get well ahead, so I won't be panicking each week, and for the better reason that I'd like to be planning well ahead regarding lesson ideas and connections and options. You can't do that if you are not ahead by at least a week. (A veteran would probably say by at least several years.) I keep a copy of each of my texts at home so I don't have to haul them around and in case I get a flash of inspiration or panic any given night. The point: The more prepared the better.

A note was delivered to the 6th (last) period teachers in my building today. It said there were rumors that there may be a fight in the hallway, so I was requested (as were all the 400 Building teachers) to stand out by the door and simply be a deterring presence. Duly summoned, we all stood by our doors bidding pleasant wishes for the students' weekends while trying to appear as authority figures heading trouble off at the pass. I guess it worked. All I saw was the usual girl hitting guy playfully and flirtfully in the shoulder, with much giggling and posturing going on. A good time was had by all.

I'm contemplating putting a sign up over my classroom door that says something to the effect that this is a "No Swearing" zone. I could write up 100 tickets during each between-period rush. Something needs to be done.

Sunday night. The weekend started Saturday at 8:00 a.m., when I left the house to coach my oldest son's soccer game — we lost, now

0-2. He and I then went to another son's game going on simultaneously in a different part of town. My wife was there and met a friend with kids. They are all going to a park after soccer. I played in a golf event that I was invited to by a new teacher/friend. I wrestled only slightly with that because I should be spending more time preparing. However, I am ready for Monday, I like to golf, and this will be the last time I play until spring.

Today didn't get any less busy. Up for church. Home for projects in the afternoon. The bulldozer is coming tomorrow to start the process of getting power installed. I spent the day cleaning around the path of the bulldozer. My evening consisted of taking the kids to a church meeting, doing laundry at the Coin-Op, (c'mon, bulldozer) going back home to pick up my wife and other kids, then back in to town for dessert at a friend's house. I snuck in 20 minutes of outlining the history book while parked in the Safeway parking lot. Grab preparation time where you can. Of course, the better plan would be to create a schedule where the preparation time has a higher priority. But for now, real life.

✎ 3rd Week: Sept. 21st - 25th

Today we had our first regular faculty meeting. I wasn't feeling well and felt like falling asleep ...The main topic was kids bringing weapons on campus ... Now I was awake.

Monday night. Today in History, we finished watching a movie about the Mayflower trip to Plymouth. It was a timely movie because that's where we are in the text. Unfortunately, it wasn't that great of a movie. As one student put it, "It was a soap opera." I'd seen that movie about two years ago and had forgotten the bad parts. I didn't preview it again and should have. It had some value, but I doubt I'll show it again. I will test on it this time, though. The students were told there would be test questions about the movie, and to encourage them to pay attention to stuff that happens in class, I should follow through with my promise (threat?).

One of my better history students complimented me today, though it may have been a veiled attempt to continue an easy routine. I was told that she liked my method of having each student report to the class on just a bit of the chapter, with all bits coming together, like one big study group. The kids pay attention, take notes, and move from the knowledge to the comprehension level. It also gets the students speaking in front of a group (from their chair), forming their thoughts, and speaking more or less extemporaneously. It could be good, I think, and so did that student. It might've also had something to do with the fact that she got a 96 on the first test. I should also point out that some complain about this method.

I'm determined to meet with the math department head this week to get some games and activities to break up the routine in class. We just go from one assignment to the next, and it's getting, well, routine. Same thing with the history classes. I want at least one day per week when we do something other than report on the chapter. That's probably why I showed the movie. At least it broke up the routine. I took the movie back to the veteran teacher's desk and noticed an activity sheet for the kids on the front table. I swiped one (with permission) to use for my class. I told her I would like to touch bases with her periodically, and borrow some of her ideas and handouts. She was all for it. That will be very helpful, though I won't know ahead of time what's going to be available. I hinted — no — confessed, that I'd like to go over all her handouts with her. It's not her job to teach my classes, but she has invited me to review her stuff anytime. I'm fortunate to have that help.

I did an "assumptions" paper in Teen Law today. The kids were given a statement that called to mind an obvious assumption or presumption. The assignment was for them to come up with a different, unexpected reason why a certain event took place. As they were talking among themselves, they were actually discussing the assignment. Even though I'd told them not to talk and to do their own work, I felt good that they felt compelled to talk about the assignment. That was better than silence.

More administrative advances. I made photo copies of my seating charts. They're up at the podium all the time. I don't have to take them out of my master notebook each period. Also, I made a copy of the key to the filing cabinet and put the spare in a different part of the room. Paranoid? I don't know, but I do have tests, answer keys, ongoing lesson plans and the grade book in there, and I'd hate to lose them.

Tuesday night. Today I arranged for a teacher across the hall to rush in to my teen law class, do something sudden, and rush out. The kids were to be tested on details of what they saw. They all came up with different answers for his shirt and hair color, what he said and what he threw to me. It was more fun than I had planned and it showed the fallibility of eyewitness accounts. The kids enjoyed it, but the problem is, once the fun is over, what's next? Plan, plan, plan.

The principal came in during a history class to "observe." It was all going fine. I was there and no one was on fire. The kids actually were responding, sort of.

I am finding that giving tests has a lot of angles. I am allowing those who do real poorly to do a re-take. I am not interested in flunking a non-worker. My goal is to keep him on it until he does it right. I was told there should be three grades: A, B and Not Yet. I'll stick with that principle but throw C in as a fourth option. One kid who got a 24 (out of 100) told me he didn't intend to re-take the test, that he'd just live with it. I'll be talking with him first, then call his parents if need be. There are a few others just like him I hope to follow up on.

Conducting a lecture/discussion in front of the class is hard. I pit out. I really want kids to be enthused, participate and be on task more than they are. I'll be thinking of discussion topics to liven things up. Today's topic was, "Would you leave your society and go to a new

land if one were discovered?" It was a follow-up on the pilgri
got 'em going a little bit regarding freedom, laws, and life ir
in general.

It was a good discussion and accomplished about everything I want
to do in my class discussions. There was wide involvement, the topic
sparked high interest, it allowed the students to feel they had a stake
in something, and it was related to the subject matter we were covering.

One student was encouraged that I noticed in the paper she participated in a cross-country meet. It also opened a line of discussion with
that student. This shouldn't be surprising, but I'm discovering that
the kids are like all of us. We like it when someone takes the time to
know a little about us, to show an interest.

Wednesday night. We are having the power put in. We are the proud
owners of a 1,400-foot ditch, 4 feet deep. And today it started pour-
ing. There is a lot of mud, and we have no driveway. Meanwhile, I'm
suppose to find time to prepare for school.

In Teen Law, I gave the kids their first test. The format is like History, with matching and short essays. To construct the test, I simply go
over my notes and the text, pick out key words and concepts, and
figure out which I want to use in the matching and which in the short
essays. I make each short essay worth about twice each matching question. I'm not stuck on that though, and I sense some changes there.

For my history classes, I have given the kids a biography assignment. They are to read a book about an American of their choosing
from the time period we are studying. Today I got to school a bit early
and remembered that this was the day I had reserved the library for my
history classes to work on this biography assignment. I had told them
they would be doing a biography, but gave vague details. In a last-
minute fit of professionalism I felt they needed some written direction.
I went to the teachers' lounge, where I found the word processor vacant. I was able to compose a detailed instruction sheet, printed it out,
and ran up to the copy room behind the library. I made my 90 copies
and made it to my first period class just about on time. The whole
hurried morning reminded me of the first day of classes.

The additional reason for having the sheet is that for the next several hours or days, I won't have to repeat the instructions for the
twenty-umpteenth time. "Here, read the sheet."

A student in a later class told me I was his favorite teacher. He's a
nice kid, but the factors he'd use to determine a good teacher are not

exactly what my professors had in mind. Something to do with a combination of listening to the kids and allowing snacks. Anyway, I take it as a compliment, and maybe I can make some progress with him. Also in the "progress hopeful" department, a kid who had been suspended for a week took a test on the things we covered while he was gone. He got 20 out of 100. I give re-tests to allow the students to try to get a C+, so I told him I'd give him my notes to study and use on the retake. He's a bit older, this is his third try to pass U.S. History, and I want to do the extraordinary if it will help. We had a nice chat about what he needs to do. We'll see what happens.

Today we had our first regular faculty meeting. I wasn't feeling well and felt like falling asleep. Maybe sleeping at a faculty meeting doesn't have anything to do with not feeling well. Anyway, the main topic was kids bringing weapons on campus and what we can do. Now I was awake. Basically, the message was to report anything you see or hear. Mercifully the principal cut the meeting short, and we were out by 3:30. I say mercifully because I had to hustle home and make sure the power and phone lines were getting installed.

I'm wrestling with what to do with kids who don't turn in work on time. I will be giving them some credit, but not as though it was in on time. I should come up with some written policy on this for unexcused lateness.

There are many such administrative concerns. I wonder how life downtown would be if they allowed the concept of an "excused lateness?"

"Joe, that was the third time you've been late this week. You're fired!"

"Sorry, Mr. Watson, but you can't do that. Each one was excused. See, I have a note."

Some teachers at lunch mentioned that if the students miss a certain number of classes their grade is reduced. I disagree, thinking the grade is a separate issue from attendance sanctions and other discipline matters. I didn't speak up, being the new guy and all.

Friday night, end of third week. Today in History/Gov't. I improvised — had the students break into groups of three or four and work on section review questions. Had it due in 35 minutes. That made them actually work on the assignment, not to mention that it was five points per participant. They then reported their answers to the whole class. It was just another way of breaking the routine yet getting through the material.

Some of the Seniors in the math class were really getting crude in their discussion of their personal sex lives. They were talking among themselves, but very aware that they were loud enough to be heard by everyone. I spoke up and told them to change the subject. One of the boys tried to claim his free speech rights, but I reminded him that I was in charge of the room and I would stop any loud discussions which were inappropriate.

Right after that, for the second time this year, my department head walked in while the kids (and I) were seemingly doing nothing. The reason we were seemingly doing nothing is that we were actually doing nothing. It was Friday and they had plowed through the assignments this week. I gave them a review assignment, not mandatory, to help them get ready for the next test. Not mandatory, I should know by now, is akin to not at all.

Today is our 10th wedding anniversary, so I took off in the middle of the day, during my planning period, and went downtown to have a locket engraved. It felt strange leaving campus during the day, as though I was cheating or something. Maybe I was. Anyway, I got my chore done and got back in time. It worked out fine, and served as a reminder that there is life going on "out there."

I'll be an assistant basketball coach, and today the head coach talked about duties for the upcoming season. It'll be here soon. I'm looking forward to it, but my wife will not be glad about the time I'll be away from the family. That is a conflict that will be coming. I don't think there is a solution, just compromise and understanding on both sides.

In most of my classes, I feel a rapport developing. The kids are getting a sense of my approach and sense of humor, and hopefully appreciating what I have to offer. It's amazing how some don't pay attention, though. It seems I have to give simple directions several times. I'll refuse to repeat them someday soon, and see if that causes them to pay more attention.

This evening, prior to the Big Game, we attended a town barbecue in an area adjacent to the football field. Lots of people, small town atmosphere, very fun. I hope to plug in and become better friends with many of these people before too long.

4th Week: Sept. 28th - Oct. 2

Today I had my first confrontation with a student. Well, it wasn't a confrontation, but it was a situation where I was faced with either doing something or losing the respect of the class. One student was continually chatting, and I mentioned that if he kept talking, he'd have to move. He immediately made some more comments to his neighbor, so there I was ...

Monday night. I went to a law office today and got some "Advance Sheets," which are booklets containing law cases in Washington (also a great name for a sailboat). I will give these to my law class tomorrow to show them what a written legal opinion looks like.

I should point out that before the year began, I introduced myself around the courthouse, so I knew some of the judges. I was given the name of an attorney in town who likes to, or at least is willing to, speak to high school classes, and I have spoken with him. You can't have too many resources.

It seems that in my history and math classes, I struggle to have enough material to fill the hour. In Law, I am just getting into the material and the class is already over. There are too many side stories, but I hope that makes the class fun. I think what that points out is that the broader knowledge and experience base you can bring into a class, the better it will be. You have much more to offer, know the beginning from the end, and can confidently head off into any direction at any time, or relate one topic to another. That, I think, describes me in my law class. It does not describe me in my history classes, except when we can relate whatever issue we are discussing to something current. I need to be studying additional history resources.

In one class, for some reason the fallacy of "safe sex" came up for discussion. I pointed out that condoms don't always prevent disease, and don't always prevent pregnancy. One guy seemed shocked by what I was saying. I sensed he was mad at me because it was obvious that some of the girls were listening, and I may've been cutting in on his action. Actually, that's probably not the case, but there is something satisfying about thinking that.

Regarding the confrontation mentioned above, when the student continued talking, the class became absolutely quiet, focused on the unfolding drama. If I had let it go, I would've been telling the class that I wasn't able to maintain reasonable order, and that I wasn't keeping my word. So I told him to pack his stuff and move to a different spot away from his friends. We were staring at each other. He got up and moved. He cockily shoved his new desk into the front of the desk behind him and leaned back into that person's space. I had NO trouble immediately telling him to put the desk back where it was and to get out of the space of the fellow behind him. That wasn't optional on my part. I needed to take immediate action to protect the other student.

Now, what if he hadn't moved to the new chair? I would've given the class something to work on, which they wouldn't have, and have quietly gone over and asked him to join me in the hall for a talk. I'd tell him that we had a situation, and it wasn't a power struggle or anything like that. The reason it's not a power struggle is because between teacher and student, there is no issue as to where the power is. If I let him "win" in that situation, I would have 30 students doing whatever they want, and that's not how it works. If he forced me to call the discipline office to have him removed physically, I would've advised him that I won't do that, that I'd rather have him sit where he wanted for his last hour ever in my class, realizing that starting tomorrow, he wouldn't be there, and wouldn't get a needed credit. You need to have an administration that backs you on that, and I believe I have that. I also believe that a teacher needs to have reasonable and sensible rules and applications of those rules in the first place in order to command a reasonable level of respect and cooperation.

He was fine for the rest of the class across the room. He actually participated in the Q and A part of the class. I will see how he is tomorrow.

Tuesday night. I met with the basketball coach today. I will be assisting in the program somewhere, and we briefly discussed that he would be wide open for advice and suggestions. He is very open and friendly. The only problem that creeps in is the time that will be required to be away from my family. Well, that, and the fact that I've never coached basketball before. I have played high school and some college ball though, and very much want to coach. I am looking forward to it.

The discipline issue from yesterday has apparently been resolved. He was much quieter today. That could be because we had a test for the full period, but I'll claim a good improvement for the class anyway.

We had a department meeting for Social Studies after school. There are eight in the department, ranging in experience from about 34 years on down to Yours Truly, who at this time has about three weeks in. The meeting was informal and short. There was a discussion of some issues in the curriculum. The Social Studies department is up for review next year and we need to focus on developing an updated statement of goals and objectives. Also, we will be buying new texts at the end of next year, so we need to begin selecting samples to preview in next year's classes. I was impressed at how everyone got to the issues, discussed them and got on. Frankly, everyone is anxious to get out of there after school.

I just devised a test for Chapter 2 in History. It is very different from my first test because I included mostly short answer. I am going to have them work on vocabulary words in class tomorrow, and turn them in. That will be part of the test. I feel good about this test because it is all mine.

Wonderful things happen unexpectedly. At home, in addition to having the power lines installed, we are planting a lawn. I need rock rakers to help me prepare it for seeding. I'm using a program at school which locates kids who need the money for things such as a band trip. This evening I called the lady in charge of the program, and I was directed to go to the marching band practice and talk to her there. It was at the parking lot of the stadium, under the lights. While at the practice, I saw a number of "my kids" practicing very diligently. It was hard to describe the feeling I had when I saw them working hard, being conscientious about their performance. There are several kids I wouldn't suspect would be that committed. My respect for them soared tonight. I had unintentionally labeled some kids in a certain way, and I was wrong.

With the good, earlier today there was a negative. I used the history class periods to have the kids do a rote vocabulary assignment. You know, look up all the vocabulary words at the end of the chapter. One of my better students didn't like that assignment, thought it was unimaginative and told anyone who would listen. Unfortunately, I have to agree. It will help them on the test, but it was a bit of a "punt" on my part. I will constantly have to be on the search to find, make or steal ideas for exciting lessons. On the flip side of that, I realize no one always hits home runs, and I will not burn out with self-criticism. Just keep plodding, with some invention where you can.

I got my first check today. This is going to be interesting. As I walked away from the bookkeeper's office with the check, I caught myself thinking that if this were doubled, I could survive about right. We'll see what's in store. I admit to wondering what I could do for supplemental income.

Thursday night. Today I got a big boost from an unexpected source. About seven weeks ago, out of anger, I wrote to a major TV personality about how sleazy some of the stuff on a certain show was. He actually wrote back and agreed with me. I read the letter to students in my current events and history classes as an impetus for them to take stands on issues. They were impressed that I got a response. They listened intently as I read the letter — quietest the room has been all year — and some said, "Good for you" as I was reading. And it broke up the routine a bit.

I gave the history test. Mostly short answer questions. I got some very short answers. The kids said they liked the matching ones better. I realized that it's easier to make up a short-answer (essay) test than it is to grade it. Just like it's harder to make a matching test and easier to grade it.

Friday night. Today I had better history classes. We are about to head into the chapter on the American Revolution, so, without the kids being told why, I had them break up in groups and come up with an issue where a person or a group of people have been treated unfairly, and how could the problem have been averted or solved. In each of the three periods, the kids dove into the assignment and came up with some exciting, heated examples.

The issues they came up with were discrimination against women; discrimination against men when there is an allegation of sexual harassment; discrimination against arrest victims by overly zealous police; prejudice against police when someone alleges a false arrest; discrimination against youth, against gays, against AIDS victims, against students and other oppressed groups. Solutions ranged from taking personal actions for self-help to working toward changing attitudes in society through better education and communication.

It made me wish the principal was standing there observing as he does occasionally. He wasn't, but that's how it goes.

On the flip side, I had a very weak math class today. Then again, I didn't get observed, so I guess it worked out. In Math, the kids had just taken a test and have been doing an assignment a day, so they talked me into not giving them one that was due right away, it being Friday and all. I gave in. I made it due at the end of Monday's class. The result of that was that just about no one was doing any work in class. The few who were got my attention and help, but I caught myself looking over my shoulder hoping that none of my superiors would walk in the door. None did. In my defense, there is a 180-day schedule on how to proceed through the book, and we are ahead of schedule. However, I should have alternate plans available and present them so the kids will want to participate.

Tomorrow I'm doing the raking project at my house. I've arranged for four students to come and help for a half-day on Saturday. The four were randomly assigned by the music department because the music kids need to raise funds for a field trip to Carnegie Hall. I'm looking forward to interacting with the kids outside the school setting.

I got a gradebook program for the computer. This is one thing I should've done before the first day of class. I need to figure out how to use it, then get my grades on the system. The first advisory grades are due in two weeks, and I'm not ready. I have been told that even though the set-up takes time, a computer is very valuable at the end of the semester, when the list of entries gets unmanageable if done by hand.

✒ 5th Week: Oct. 5 -9

The boy in history class who was doing nothing is now doing something: transferring to the alternative high school. I received his official withdrawal papers today. I didn't really do or say anything to help or encourage him. My job isn't to be here to see if I can survive. It's to help the kids, however broadly that gets defined. Do it while you can. I'm learning.

Monday night. This morning I remembered that I had ordered two videos to review for my law class. Videos are ordered by filling out a form that lists what you want and the date you want it. The librarian sends it to the Educational Service District, and you may or may not get the film, depending on if it has already been reserved. So, you need two plans, depending on if the film comes in. The ones I ordered arrived.

I knew one of them, *Gideon's Trumpet*, was good. I had seen it several years ago, but didn't remember if it had objectionable parts. I previewed it and found that it's a good movie showing not only the issue at hand (the right of an accused to have an attorney), but a good look at the court and appeal process. This will have high appeal for the kids because it satisfies some basic criteria the kids are looking for: It's an actual movie, not a documentary; it's in color; it's a true story; and it's about something the kids can believe they may have a stake in.

As I hope to do for any movies I show, I have devised a few pages of simple questions for the kids to answer while they are watching. My goal is to keep them focused and thinking about what is going on.

I'm still amazed at how some kids buzz among themselves during class. I don't blame them, because that's part of being 14 or 15 years old. It seems like there is a 10 year difference between freshmen and juniors. Sophomores are somewhere in the middle.

Our school sets the schedule of classes according to who signs up. If no one signs up for a class, then that class doesn't get taught. In my case, Teen Law is the elective I'd like to see a lot of kids sign up for, because I enjoy teaching it, and it's my area of expertise. Therefore I impliedly — no, make that explicitly — recruit for that class.

This is Homecoming Week. Today we had an assembly dealing with selecting a king and queen from each class, that type of thing. Back in class afterward there was some discussion about whether a person who has one honor or selected position, such as cheerleader, should also be allowed to be royalty. Overtly the issue was fairness; covertly it was envy.

This week is also Dress Weird Week. That has some hidden humor, because around our campus, there is no real dress code, and every week might as well be Dress Weird Week. Anyway, today was Opposite Sex Day, tomorrow is Pajama day, then Hawaiian day, etc. Tomorrow I'll wear my Hawaiian shirt which I sometimes sleep in, killing two birds with one stone.

I am making progress getting the grades onto the computer. They are due at the end of next week, and I don't have them ready yet. I need to get that done.

It's clear that some kids don't listen to simple directions. Some don't have any idea I'm even giving a direction because I'm simply not what they're focusing on. They socialize instead of listen. Like I said, they're 14, or 16, and that's what they do. I can't get upset with them, or with myself, because they're not in total awe of what I'm saying all the time. I guess the best I can say is that if I have not prepared or don't have a good lesson, the kids will be bored and not tune in. If I have a great lesson going, loaded with fun and wisdom, the kids might notice, but I shouldn't worry if they don't. I need patience and thick skin. I should point out that most of the time in all my classes, the kids are attentive and trying.

Teachable moments come at odd times. One of my math students asked what I thought when someone in the next car gives you the finger. Okay, its not exactly a math question, but it does have to do with digits. We talked about feeling sorry for someone who walks (or drives) around with the weight of hate on them, and how their immaturity shouldn't cause you to react with immaturity. That seemed to spark the student to think about that scene completely differently than before. A follow-up discussion ensued and it made my hour.

I'll be going to a basketball seminar this weekend. We have started open gym this week, and I had to be a no-show for my first time as supervisor. It was with prior approval of the head coach, who reiterated that it was no big deal because it's not a formal turnout anyway, and sometimes we just won't be able to be there. He was very under-standing and encouraging, but I feel bad about missing my first unofficial coaching duty.

One kid in History is doing absolutely nothing. No, I take that back. He's breathing. I think. If there were a grade worse than F he'd have it. I've talked with him several times. I need to call his home to inform them what he told me — that he intends to do nothing, and he is going to transfer to the alternative school anyway. Let's see tomorrow if I call his parents.

I turned in my Substitute Folder today. It was due a while ago, but I kept not doing it because I didn't know what form it was suppose to take. I eventually asked and was told to do whatever I wanted. My substitute experience came in handy here because I know what I liked when I showed up to sub: clear instructions, papers where they were suppose to be, names of kids I could rely on in each class, and a strong statement from the teacher to the kids that if anyone tries to take ad-vantage of the sub, there will be consequences because we all know the games. Also, if there's an assignment the sub can actually DO with the kids, it beats babysitting. Almost always, I was instructed just to babysit while the kids worked on an assignment.

I like my test re-take policy. The kids are forced to review the mate-rial, and they can get up to 75 points on a retake. Given that a few of them get in the 20 to 40 range (out of 100) the first time around, this is a good opportunity for them to do a couple things: raise their grade so they are still in the ball game, and secondly, get involved, since they know they are still in the game, they may not lose heart. One kid I've got falls into that category, and it's encouraging to see him pay atten-tion.

I was in my class early today (about 6:00), and the principal walked in. I guess it feels good to get noticed being there early, but all I was doing was correcting papers which I should've done some other time during the weekend. We talked about the year, and I mentioned that my cold is getting thicker and I'm tired and plugged up. He said that October is a rough time on new teachers. I normally have excellent health, but being exposed to the collective germs of a high school could cause a problem. Or maybe it already has.

Speaking of health, or the lack of it, I've caught myself continuing one routine. After 2nd period, I go over to the cafeteria and grab a cup of coffee and a half a roll (or whatever the cafeteria staff leaves on the lunch table for snacks) and hustle back to my room for 3rd period. It is a fun thing to do in the middle of the morning.

Thursday night. I've just completed putting my math grades on computer. Having it calculate percentages and update the grades at the press of a button is a lifesaver. I'm sure that in the near future all teachers will be doing this and it will be absurd to even mention it. But for now, some don't use a computer. I highly recommend it. I will show the kids the printout and some will be disappointed in their grade. Hopefully they'll be shocked into action.

The boy in history class who was doing nothing is now doing something: transferring to the alternative high school. I received his official withdrawal papers today. I didn't really do or say anything to help or encourage him. My job isn't to be here to see if I can survive. It's to help the kids, however broadly that gets defined. Do it while you can. I'm learning.

Friday night. Since this was Friday of Homecoming Week, not much work was expected to get done today. The classes were shortened because of a pep assembly in the morning. The band was there, getting the kids all hyped up. We teachers and administrators tried to make sure the kids stayed slightly calmed down. This year, the school administration didn't allow the boys to have a tug-of-war because last year a riot nearly broke out. The compromise was to have a girls' tug-of-war. It was fun and loud, but there needed to be "security" to keep the guys back.

Because of the short schedule and all the activity, one administrator said, "Any learning that takes place today is strictly accidental." I'm glad I wasn't the only one who felt that way. Anyway, in History I did have one thing planned — to have a student read an article about a topic we were covering that had just appeared in the paper. It made for a brief discussion, and that was it. I mention that because the principal stopped in for a visit during that discussion. Whenever that happens, it causes me to be acutely aware of whether or not I have something appropriate, or better, going on.

There are many times when the kids will put pressure on me to be a good guy and allow them a special privilege, usually in the form of permission to go on an errand. The teacher is liable if something happens to the student. Also, in addition to lost class time, it sets a bad precedent. And, it is against school rules. I need to remember that because I get those types of requests a lot. Are they just preying on the new guy?

The last period of the day (History/Government) on Fridays is turning into a debate class on social issues like gun control, child-support levels, abortion, and censorship. I love it, but in the midst of these fun discussions, I need to remember a couple things: to keep this class up with my other two History classes; to connect the discussions to the topics we are suppose to be covering; and to remind myself I am dealing with 16 year olds and need to see these discussions from their perspectives.

I took my two older sons to the BIG GAME tonight. We won, and my kids actually enjoyed the whole game (and the snack breaks). When it was over, I went down to where the band was seated and congratulated one of my students, one of the band leaders, on a job well done. This will sound silly, but he hasn't had it easy, has accomplished many things, and I was proud of him. Along the way in the stands I got a lot of, "Hi Mr. Gish!" from the kids. Knowing I have the opportunity to be a positive influence for these kids is a wonderful but scary feeling.

Sunday night. This weekend I went to my first basketball coaches' clinic. I am scheduled to be Sophomore boys' coach, so I want to plug in where I can as soon as I can. I was looking forward to this because one of the reasons I got into teaching was to coach.

The boys' head coach, his assistant and I went to Seattle for the clinic, which ran from Saturday morning to Sunday afternoon. The speakers were big-time nationally known coaches: Dean Smith, Hubie Brown, and Denny Crum. All were entertaining, but presented a little too many Xs and Os for me. Actually, my favorite speaker was a woman who coaches an extremely successful girls' team at a Seattle high school. No Xs and Os, just a lot on motivation and the personal side of the world of coaching.

I don't know if it is fair or not, but in recent years, I've compared the seminars and clinics I attended on how to win a lawsuit with the sports clinics my friends who coach talked about. From their descriptions, I guessed that the coaches clinics were just as useful and a lot more fun than the legal seminars. I was right.

Over the weekend I learned from the head coach that our program is coming off a rough year. "The basketball season from hell," he said.

Kids with poor attitudes were causing problems, and that sort of thing. As he and I discussed, I'll write him a note with my rookie thoughts about how we can have a successful program. I was no star player, but in high school I played (rather, sat the bench) in a very disciplined program, where the coaches commanded and received much respect. I will simply be trying to repeat what went on there because I have no other experience to draw from, and I'll tell him that. I can be idealistic this month — before the season starts.

After returning from the basketball clinic, I went to school for a few hours to get all my grades on my computer disk. Grades are due at the end of next week and I'm almost ready. A problem is that some kids haven't turned stuff in, so they have some "0"s which skew their grade. I hope they make up the work. I don't want to be faced with giving an F to a kid. A selfish reason I don't want that is because if I'm giving out Fs I should've called their parents long ago to address the problem. I'm just hoping to solve the problem by giving opportunities for make-up work to come in.

I'm also kind of sick — have had a bad cold for ten days. I can't hear well in class. The one thing I fear is being sick. I want to be involved all year — healthy — so I can give teaching a fair try. I'll call for a Dr. appointment tomorrow. I guess the principal was right about October.

I'm going to a drug-abuse clinic tomorrow, all day. There is a substitute arranged for me, and that brings up a range of feelings. First, have I left clear enough instructions for the sub? Are the tasks the kids will be doing each period appropriate to our flow in the class, or did I just come up with some busy-work to make the sub's day go okay? Will the sub come in to my room and discover I'm not well-prepared for weeks in advance? In other words, maybe I'm not proud enough of my job of preparing. I would say that's slightly the case, but not entirely. Some of my best lessons have come from last-minute changes in plans to deal with current events which relate to a topic we are dealing with.

✒ 6th Week: Oct. 12th - 16th

I discovered that my timing in History was not great. I finished the chapter on Tuesday and earlier announced the test would be on Thursday. So what to do Wednesday? I could give them time to review, but that feels like I'm wasting time. I've got about ten hours — it's 9:00 p.m. — to come up with a meaningful alternative to an air ball.

Monday night. This morning I went in early to get my room ready for the substitute. The seminar I was attending didn't start until the middle of 1st period, about 8:30 in human time, so I started class and talked with the sub. I felt that I hadn't prepared enough for the day. Preparing for a substitute is very hard because it forces you to write in detail what you would be doing by instinct or habit. Teaching is the only job I know that's harder if you're not going to be there. I got the kids started, but they were chatting away while I was leaving.

At lunch break during my seminar, I came back to my room to see how things were going. There was a note from the substitute to me indicating that the kids really weren't working on their assignments, but just chatting, with a few exceptions. In one class I gave an assignment for them to work on and they all finished it within about 15 minutes. I guess I didn't have it timed quite right.

Timing a lesson plan to last precisely 50 minutes requires a finely tuned ability in a very sensitive area: Guessing. So far I haven't had to worry much about the timing because I've been following along the text, and if I have more time left over at the end of my plan, I can (but rarely have done so) simply keep going in the text. Finishing the hour before going through the intended material is a rare treat.

The seminar was about how to handle drug use by students who are involved in extracurricular activities. The method discussed is picking a captain of the team or club to be the role model, and who will help monitor and correct violations. The goal is drug-free kids; the method is to have peer role models.

After the seminar, I checked my room. The substitute's notes were about the same for the afternoon classes as for the morning.

I prepared for tomorrow's classes. Preparing for classes goes something like this: In History I review the specific sections we'll be going over and prepare discussion topics or a worksheet. During class I'm at the overhead helping students talk about their assigned sections and writing key thoughts. Two problems with that: First, when students are reporting, they talk very softly and fast, so I have to repeat everything, and second, my handwriting on the overhead is a constant source of bad jokes or just plain frustration for many students.

Law class goes much the same, except during the lecture, the kids are more drawn into the discussion.

After I finished preparing (can you ever be done?), I went to open gym. I was in charge of getting the balls in and out of the equipment room, and kicking the kids out at 5:00. We really can't coach yet, so there's not much of that. Just watching. I did some school work, too.

I called to make a doctor appointment. My "cold" is in its second week, and I'm getting more plugged, hoarse and hard of hearing by the day. I don't want it to turn into pneumonia, so I'm being cautious.

Grades are due next Monday. Friday is an in-service day, no classes, just workshops for the teachers. Maybe I'll have some time to get my grades done. I've got them all on disk, so I feel ready. The part that I feel a bit behind about is that some kids need to get in late work or re-take a test to get a passing grade, and I want to make sure they do that.

Tuesday night. Today we finished going through Chapter Three in the history text. I'm hoarse, and in my law class, my voice broke a few times during the lesson, bringing giggles from some. Then something happened out of the blue that I learned a lot from.

One of the kids said something sort of snide to me, so I said something sort of snide back. No big deal, no confrontation, but I felt bad for forgetting for a second I was dealing with a 9th grader, who has concerns other than impressing teachers with politeness all the time.

I learned a lesson from that. Take fun and positive comments personally. Weigh the others slowly and be thankful if you can sift out suggestions on how your teaching might improve. Then move on.

Today we had what is called a "bus drill." I had to ask the kids what it was. The reply: "A stupid drill, where you learn how to jump out of the side door of a bus." They said most of them rarely take the bus anyway, so it was stupid. Until you're in a bus emergency, I guess.

If we are supposed to be getting nervous about the first open house, which is tomorrow night, I'm missing out on that emotion. In fact, I had to go back to check my schedule to make sure it is tomorrow night, because I had just filed it back in my brain somewhere. It is, and

I expect about 20 parents out of 140 to show up. We'll see. Am I suppose to have a lesson plan ready? Maybe I should give homework due on the next open house?

It is the middle of the 6th week, and we just finished Chapter One in Teen Law. I am proud of that because I've taken lots of side trips and have been able to plug in my knowledge to supplement or even correct the text. In History, as I mentioned, we just finished the third chapter. It's probably a fair extrapolation to say I know about three times as much about the law material as I do about history. That's why I've gone faster through History, relying on and sticking closer to the text. I need to go more efficiently through both, I guess.

Thursday night. Last night was open house. The theory is that the parents can come and meet the teachers and see what's going on in school. I was a bit curious about how many parents would show up, so I asked one of the veteran teachers, who said usually about one-fifth of the kids would be represented, or less. Another teacher said it depends on how good the teacher is. The better the teacher, the more parents will show up. According to his theory, I'm a lousy teacher. I had about three kids per class represented by one or two parents. He had about fifteen kids per class. However, I don't feel too defeated. I was not surprised to learn that my numbers are typical, and the only classes which get more parents are the college-bound classes. The parents who did show up in my classes were the parents of the better students. The parents you wish would show up simply are not interested. No surprises there. Anyway, I basically explained how I conduct class, how I test, re-test, and try to have all my classes connected to real life. It all was very polite and predictable. Afterward, however, I noticed some profanity which students had scrawled on a few of the texts which the parents had been looking at.

One parent was concerned because her child didn't seem to have much homework in my classes. I guess that's true. One surprise I've had this year is how many kids work after school between 20 and 40 hours per week. I better get most, if not all, of the information out during class time or they may not get it at all. I am concerned that I am teaching too much to the middle — or lower — student.

A major victory in Math today. One girl who, for the first few weeks, was not involved and who was in fact hostile toward me — she got angry when I mispronounced her name — and toward school in general, has turned the corner. She's experienced some success on re-takes and now realizes she could do well all the time if she wanted.

There is a lot of profanity around the school. I'm starting to make a point of calling the kids on it, asking them to clean up their language. Most of them just fake a bit of embarrassment and turn away. But like one of the administrators said, we can't just let it go. They will at least know that some segment recognizes a standard on that sort of thing.

We are having a fellow teacher and his wife over for dinner next week. His job primarily is to deal with kids who are discipline problems, and it will be interesting getting some of his stories. Also, I'd like to become closer friends with some of the teachers.

I took my two oldest kids up to the gym after school yesterday. However, girls' volleyball took over the whole place, so I just wandered around the gyms and out to football practice with my kids. I enjoyed seeing my students practicing hard and having them meet my kids. I'm becoming more convinced that the more contact you have with the kids outside of class, the better the situation will be in class.

I am also realizing that school is a place where you basically live. If you are a clock-watcher, not only will you not enjoy what's going on, you'll miss much of it. While I was at open gym, I went over to the other gym and saw that there was a girls' volleyball match about to start. I chatted with a coach, who is a fellow new teacher. It was a pleasant moment, and one more bit of bonding to the school.

I have mentioned I thought I was going to be an assistant boys' basketball coach, but I noticed an ad going out for that position. I talked to the Athletic Director, who told me to write him a note indicating my interest. I got a call later in the day from the head coach who made sure I had my "application" in. That's encouraging. I expect I will be coaching b-ball somewhere in the system.

Friday. Well, today was different. It was the first teacher "in-service" day. I don't know what those words mean, but what we did was attend a conference for something called clock hours, which you need to constantly accumulate to keep your teaching certificate. We were paid as if it were a regular day. I went to a first aid and CPR training session in the morning, and a Media in the Classroom seminar in the afternoon.

It was actually a busier day than a regular teaching day. I was required to be the student and pay attention, had no control over the schedule, and had no break period, other than lunch. It was good to be reminded of what school is like from the students' point of view.

✐ 7th Week: Oct. 19th - 23rd

If certain students don't want to do any work, they won't get any credit. That's different from kids who don't know how to work or who don't have the ability to read and retain correctly. For those, I'll bend over backwards to help. The others, I'll just help, and help again, but that's about it. Like the pizza example I gave. I'll set it out before them. If they want to eat it, great. If they don't, it's their choice.

Monday. Grades were due this morning by 7:15. No sweat, I had mine in by 7:13. I worked on updating my computer grading disk over the weekend, and ended up doing more work on Sunday evening than I thought I'd need to. About three hours. Anyway, I got them in. The grades were pretty much across the board, with the average grade, according to the computer, being about 75% in each class.

That 75% was accomplished backwards. That is, most people think of a bell curve, with a very few low grades and a very few high grades, and the bulk in the middle somewhere. Nope. In my classes, and I discovered it is true for others, there are many As, and many Ds, (only a few Fs because I bent over backwards to give people credit to get in the D range) and only a few in the middle. That is because the work is not hard. Either they do it or they don't. If they do it, a B is about guaranteed with an A very possible. If you don't, it'll be the F or D. It's up to them. However, I need to be more diligent in calling parents of those in danger of the F.

This morning at about 6:00, I saw an "open letter" taped to the front door of the school. It was critical of the head football coach. It was gone shortly thereafter, and not many, if any, students saw it. But I invented a way to stick my foot in my mouth, cleats and all. I thought the letter was public knowledge by 2nd period, so I mentioned it to one of the players. That started rumors flying, and I tried to downplay the whole thing. Nothing will come of it, but I learned about minding my own business. Incidentally, in any small town, the success of the football team is the subject of a thousand experts.

I did an exercise in my history/government and teen law classes today that worked great three out of the four periods I attempted it. It dealt with kids' positions on various social/political issues. Good debate and high interest. The point was to have the kids add up their responses and see, according to a grid, whether they were Republican, Democrat or Libertarian. Notice the principal doesn't walk in to observe when that's going on. I don't know why the lesson didn't go well in the fourth class, except that some buzzing and a lack of focus by a few people can put a damper on everyone's enthusiasm.

I finally realized that I need to be developing separate notebooks for Teen Law as well as for History. A smart person would've had it done a month before school starts. I'm seven weeks into the year and only just now am doing it. Scary. I've been riding too much on my own legal background. It's worked fine, but in order to have a chance to prepare for next semester or next year, I need to be able to see what's coming.

Last night I had open gym. I took my two oldest kids and we played games against each other. I met a kid who is a Senior, and he seemed polite. I say that because I notice that "polite" isn't a real common commodity.

I caught myself not wearing a sweatshirt that my wife and kids made for me a while ago. It has their handprints on it and says WE LOVE YOU DAD. Somehow I felt it would be not dressy enough or that I'm showing off my family. But I want to do that. As I sit here typing about it I feel stupid even thinking that it is an issue. Besides, I want to promote a pro-family image and life style.

3rd period History today disintegrated right in front of me. It's a small class (20) to start with and several students had to leave to take a test they missed last week. It didn't seem right to go over lecture notes that half the class would miss. We all did seat work. I sent one kid on a mission to the teachers' table in the back of the kitchen because it was his birthday. They gave him a cookie. Happy birthday.

I found out that one girl in my class has been gone a lot because she is in drug treatment. I never would have guessed.

Wednesday. Today we got off to a hopping start. There was a frog in the room. One of the girls caught it, amid the expected shrieks and laughs.

"Junior testing" time is coming up. I teach Juniors in my history classes, three periods a day. Two of those periods will be taken up in three upcoming days. What do I do with the one class I will still have? I want the classes to stay even, now there is no way. I don't think I could teach different "spots" in the chapter during the day. I know I'd miss stuff or double up on it. I asked a veteran how to solve the problem, and he told me the obvious — there is no solution. Just have the class that you have do enhancement-type work. There is a movie on this chapter that another teacher is using. That may be it.

I told the principal that I took a vote of one (me) and the result was that it wouldn't be fair to do any formal observations during the next week, because of the messed-up schedule. He said he'd be right in.

I wore my I LOVE DAD sweatshirt. It was a big hit with the kids. Pro-family influence? Or, is that unfair because some of these kids haven't even had a dad. Or maybe just wrong because the dad they' have they wished they didn't. It seems silly to waste print on such a seemingly irrelevant item, but I think the kids are affected by all of a teacher's communications, whether they are verbal or physical, including stuff you wear.

I told my classes I'd be available at lunch for those who need extra help. Most kids voted that they would come in sometime to get help. Encouraging.

Thursday. Two of my classes have been disrupted with six or so of the kids gone to testing. I basically didn't get anything done in any of the classes, except some make-up tests. I feel like I'm way behind. In the seventh week I'm in Chapter Four of the history book and haven't yet started Chapter Two in the law book. On some days I feel proud of that law "progress" because I feel I've got more to offer than the book. We are also spending time on the presidential election in the "current events" part of the class, so I shouldn't feel too badly. But tonight I feel behind, unorganized, and too lenient. Like I've fallen into the trap of being the kids' friend instead of their teacher.

I'm going to modify my re-take policy in History. Basically handing a 75 to anyone is not appropriate. I think I'll lower the highest possible on a re-take to 70 and slightly change the test, by taking off the matching words and instructing the kids to fill in the blank with whatever is in their notes or their brain. I'll see about telling the class that soon. Also, I shouldn't allow every test to be re-taken. Maybe half, or less. And of those, the highest grade they can get is the highest they have achieved on a non-retaken test. Or something like that.

I vow to make better progress in my history and teen law/current events class tomorrow. I'm doing all right, progress-wise, with my math class, though it is very predictable and plodding.

Tomorrow is a home football game. After my wife and I get our kids tucked in about 9:00, I think I'll go over to the after-game dance and see how it goes. The dance does not seem to be a big deal with most of the student body. But I'd like to go, if only to compare it to what it was like when I was in high school. Besides, the administrators like it when faculty members show up at stuff like that.

Friday night. Today went well because I meant business. I tried to use each minute of each class. I told the history classes that it was my fault that we are a bit behind, and the way we will solve that is by shorter tests — they liked that — so we could take it and go over it all in the same day. Also, I told them that we'd no longer be wasting time doing nothing or next-to-nothing when a certain number of the kids are gone. I think the classes do better and enjoy it more when we are cooking along.

The test re-takes are not going to be the same test as the first test. Going over the exam with the answers on a matching test means they could simply write down the letters of the answer, get them all right, and get their 75% mark. As I mentioned, I will remove the matching words from the re-take and have the kids fill in the line with a word or words. They will actually have to think. If certain students don't want to do any work, they won't get any credit. That's different from kids who don't know how to work or who don't have the ability to read and retain correctly. For those, I'll bend over backwards to help. The others, I'll just help, and help again, but that's about it. Like the pizza example I gave. I'll set it out before them. If they want to eat it, great. If they don't, it's their choice.

2nd period math is my homeroom, and where we get *Channel One*, the teen news program with ads. I like it because the kids become aware of things they'd never know about otherwise. It also makes for some political talk in class afterwards.

During homeroom today, I discovered that tonight at the after-game dance, the faculty will be giving mini-breathalyzers, by having randomly selected students chew a piece of treated paper to determine if they have been drinking. We had a good discussion about student rights vs. the desire to have an alcohol-free dance. Most object to the random testing idea, and claim they'll refuse the test and leave.

I'm getting ready for a field trip. Next Wednesday several history teachers are taking their classes to see *1492*, about Columbus. I jumped on the bandwagon. In hindsight, I don't think the field trip's that valuable. The kids can go see the movie if they want to. But, the substitutes have been secured and the buses ordered. We'll see what happens.

An assignment in current events about inappropriate ads went well. Kids actually volunteered funny or stupid ads, while being reminded about how the media attempt to inappropriately persuade people with sex, muscle or vanity.

I started criminal law today in Teen Law. I am determined to stick to an outline, with anecdotes, and get through this in an organized, efficient, fun manner. I will be preparing the notebook ahead of time — it will be more fun and much less stressful to have a set curriculum.

A fellow first-year teacher and his wife came to our house for dinner. He is sure he is meant to be teaching younger kids, and feels pretty certain that next year he won't be at the high school. It'd be tough to stick out the year knowing that decision has been made. One of the strengths I hold onto is that I feel fairly certain, as I sit here tonight on October 23, that I will be at the high school quite some time.

Next week we're having another teacher over. A veteran. I'm looking forward to two things: getting to know him better and picking his brain for innovative ideas for the classroom.

✒ 8th Week: Oct. 26th - 30th

The principal walked in for a bit to observe and all was well, if well can be defined as when one of the feistier students is practically shouting why he thinks a particular law sucks. It was animated, and that's what I want.

Monday night. A student in Teen Law asked how far we were going to get in the text. She noticed it's the eighth week and we are just starting Chapter Two. Looking at it, that sounds absurd, but we've had a variety of activities and side trips. Frankly, I believe my background has allowed us to see side trips and take them confidently where another teacher might not. Just plowing through the book hasn't been my goal. However, I do feel some duty to get through the material identified in the chapters, and using the book is one way to do that.

Today and tomorrow are Junior testing days. Again. Two of my classes are basically canceled, but with a couple non-test takers showing up. I learned I wasn't the only one without a class activity planned.

I'm still aggressively trying to avoid the conspiracy of the least, where I do the least possible, demand little and adjust my methods just to be friends with the kids. The teachers I respect most, looking back over my schooling, were ones who weren't trying to be kids' friends, but were their teachers. It's harder to be a teacher than a friend. I will be their teacher. I've mentioned this before, but I bring it up again because it is very much a source of pressure and an important problem I am trying to deal with.

I put together my notebooks for Teen Law and for U.S. History. These are the same notebooks I'd already started, but I put in all the extra material I'd been collecting along the way, like handouts, etc. The plan is to develop the notebook this year, so I'll be able pick it up next year and take off, totally organized, yet ready to insert new stuff.

We kicked off book reports in History today, with a presentation from one student. She went up to the podium; I sat in a student desk. It's a good thing to get each kid up there, earlier than I've done, to try and deal with the rumblings, talking and lack of attention sometimes shown the speaker/teacher. This student, however, is one of the best in class, and doesn't need that lesson. It's like a lot of things in school — the ones who need it, don't get it. The ones who don't, do.

Tuesday night. Today in my teen law class I just talked about the subject matter through, not over, the noise. Sometimes they quieted down and got into it, sometimes a few chatted away. I didn't really lose patience or anything. I just didn't want to be constantly urging them to be quiet. Some of the other kids did, though. Finally, after class, I talked with three perpetrators, telling them I'd move them if they continued to talk in class. They seemed to take the news somberly. I suppose I should've done that during the hour. But there was nothing major and I wanted to avoid a public confrontation, so I did it this way. Let's see what happens tomorrow.

As an aside, we are discussing crimes. Today — murder and assault, things you'd think would be fairly high on the interest scale compared with much of what goes on in school. In spite of the high-interest subject matter, some kids still want to buzz among themselves. I just need to continue to realize I'm doing an okay job, that kids will be kids, so not to take stuff personally, but take at least reasonable, minimal steps to keep the class functioning.

Tomorrow is the field trip to *1492*. How many kids will actually show up? How many who don't show up at the bus will actually go to the library like they're supposed to? By the way, I told the librarian about my plan of sending the non-field trippers to the library. Justifiably, she wasn't thrilled. The proper protocol would be to send them to a different place in school, or to get a sub if there are a certain number of students who will be left behind. (There should only be a few, so a sub isn't called for) Good thing for having a flexible librarian.

I had a handout ready for history class that dealt with the history of Liberty. It had some references to personal faith. I ran that by a veteran, who told me that if I was going to use the handout, I should offer it as a balance to a different, secular view of liberty. The way I solved it was to modify the handout from faith language to "hope" language. It did no real damage to the lesson of the handout, and went a long way to eliminate a charge of "preaching."

A few kids and I had a death penalty discussion during a lull at the end of one class and before the next. Different opinions were shared in a very adult manner. There's hope for those guys.

During open gym, I played a game of CAT with one of my students. She beat me.

Wednesday. Today we went to the movie — three teachers, a counselor and about 200 students. I was in charge of one bus. We had to load the bus and get to the theater quickly, which meant we had to collect money along the way. All went well collecting the $1.50 from each person, until one girl paid in pennies. There's always one. I was stuffing the money in my pockets as I went down the aisle. Hopefully kids weren't unstuffing them as I went by. The movie, by the way, sparked interesting questions about Columbus. Good guy or bad guy?

On my first day of class, some eight weeks ago, someone asked if I had the remote control to my VCR in my room. I didn't, and no one knew where it was. Today, late October, the discipline Vice-Principal hands it over to me explaining that it had been stolen last year and had been recovered. I didn't ask too many questions.

I had a talk with a foreign exchange student. She said school here is much better than in her country. That's the first time I heard that. She said basically that the public schools in Brazil, where she's from, were non-existent. Either you went to a private school, or you didn't get an education.

I now am having trouble reconciling my several history classes. My 6th period class is way ahead, so we did nothing today, except talk about the movie. This in the face of my speech about having to go faster. Maybe it's kind of like a diet. Next week.

I am contemplating having some sort of set schedule for each week in order to catch up. It's odd that I feel like I need to catch up because I'm slightly ahead of the other history teachers. Anyway, the plan might be something like being at the same place in each chapter on Monday, then Tuesday, etc. and take the test each Friday. Something like that. I was hoping to avoid that, in the name of variety and innovation. Looks like words like "plodding" and "routine" aren't all that bad.

Tomorrow the kids in Law/Current Events will pick their candidate from among Bush, Clinton or Perot, and get their ammo ready for the "debate" on Friday. It'll be as good or bad as they want it to be.

Thursday. I started the day at 6:45, at a local church for a Fellowship of Christian Athletes meeting. There were about ten kids and a few coaches. I hope to make it a regular part of my schedule for several reasons, including what I mentioned before — any time you have contact with kids outside class, it'll help things in class.

In my law class, I moved one of the chatty students to a different part of the room. It helped her pay attention, helped her former neighbors pay attention, and the room was quieter. I was more relaxed. The principal walked in for a bit to observe and all was well, if well can be defined as when one of the feistier students is practically shouting why he thinks a particular law sucks. It was animated, and that's what I want. We had a brief discussion about some sex crimes in that class today. The class got a bit serious. I allowed those to be excused who wanted to. You never know about the background of your students, and there may be some victims there. I covered those crimes very briefly and generally, but some graphic language is necessary, because it's part of the statute.

I devised the next test in History this evening. Next year I may eliminate this chapter, or just skim it myself. I can see I'm falling way behind on the calendar, and I need to pick it up. Skipping a chapter might help. I guess the question comes in about speed vs. depth. I think my principal would vote depth. I'm not sure I'm even achieving that, but I am sure it has been slow. I want to go faster, and have less wasted time. I've been stopping with about ten minutes left in class sometimes, and I want to keep going until about two minutes left. I think that's a bit of an art that I haven't got yet. Until I do, I'll just plod along until a couple minutes to go.

Tomorrow is pay day. I can't be getting paid again already — I haven't stopped laughing at the first check yet.

Friday night. During lunch, the kids who use my room taped a kid to a chair against his will. I happened to see him on campus just at the end of lunch and he told me what happened, showed me his reddened wrists, and I could tell it wasn't a joke. They had done things like this to him before which he had joked about. I took him to the discipline vice principal who then dealt with the issue. When I went to my class, I noticed wads and strips of tape. I felt like the Vice Principal should have them in case this turned into a big deal. Or even a little deal. I wrestled with whether I was making a mountain out of a mole hill, but I felt that wasn't for me to decide. Just get the facts to the person who deals with those issues and let her decide. I did the right thing. Of course, the victim wanted nothing done, afraid of retribution. But, at least the matter's being dealt with.

I was gym monitor after school. One of the football players got hurt playing basketball while the football team was waiting for the team bus. He got a good cut on his nose. My lack of ability in first aid came shining through. The guy who got hurt is in my class, is a good kid,

51

and is someone with whom I have a good rapport. He didn't want the incident reported to anyone. He held a wet cloth on his nose, and the bleeding did stop. I cleaned the blood off the floor. I told him I didn't know what to do about his injury, but I had had similar cuts and it looked split so it would probably need stitches. But the bleeding had stopped, and he wanted to go to the game. I had to do my job, I told him that, so I took him to the locker room where there were several veteran coaches. By doing that I was admitting I didn't really know what to do, but something had to be done. One coach looked at him, told him to call his folks because he needed stitches. The coach also reminded him about not playing basketball. The kid was bummed. A few minutes later another coach taped the cut tightly closed, and the kid was allowed to go to the game. I did the right thing by taking him to a "higher authority." The next right thing would be to get more training in first aid if I'm going to be in the gym much.

In Math class I played the stereo for the first time-classical music. Some like it, some don't. Basically I won't be doing that again, because I want to keep true to my pledge of using the entire hour for class work. One idea did hit me for History. During the first few minutes of class, while I'm taking roll and people are getting settled in, I'd have a number from one of the classic musicals playing, with the words up on the overhead. Use a different musical each week. The kids will never be exposed to them otherwise. They are a snapshot of some of our history, and it'd be fun. The glitch is all the work of getting the words on a transparency, getting the cassette and the player. It's a nice idea. Let's see if it happens.

I talked with my department head about writing to a couple of places to get free, current law books and statutes. He said go for it. I'm noticing that what we have is not adequate — it's a bit dated — but there's no money to buy better material.

We had our debate in Teen Law/Current Events regarding the presidential election next week. It was rowdy, just like when adults get together to debate. I've noticed that we didn't get into the other issues or candidates on the ballot, but I don't feel bad. It was tough enough to get the kids interested in the biggy. I know I could've done more to show them the effect of the other issues on their lives, therefore cause them to be interested, but it didn't happen this time.

✎ 9th Week: Nov. 2nd - 6th

It's more like homeschooling, in that it'll be more individualized ... I guess that's my rationalization for it ... I like that ... Yes, I am inventing the wheel along the way.

Monday night. I gave a history test today — matching and short answer. The matching part entailed matching letters A through X, each representing one of the words or concepts from the chapter, to be used to match the correct phrase. The only problem was that I wrote the test while listening to the soundtrack of *Terms of Endearment,* and I had three letter D options. At least I didn't have Debra Winger as one of the answers. One of my better students complained that it was a silly mistake and was nonsense. I was embarrassed and admitted what I had done. No one really cared — it was more funny than anything. But I'll be more careful next time.

Teen law class was about out of control today. I moved a few people around, but that still didn't help. I'm talking through the noise too much. Frustrated, I went to talk to the V.P. in charge of discipline and she said of course refer them to her. It's nice to know I have that option, but I felt a little bit like a failure for asking for help or advice, because I want to have the reputation of being able to handle matters myself. However, her job is to deal with, among many other things, those types of issues. I felt better after the meeting. I will warn the perpetrators before formally "writing them up," which will result in their being sent to the V.P.'s office.

In math class, I gave back the test today. The kids did very poorly. Instead of just having them re-take it, I helped them and had them work on the ones they got wrong. I told them I didn't know how I'd re-grade it, but that it would help them to make the corrections. Most of the students did the fixing quickly, and several told me they felt silly for making simple, lack-of-patience mistakes. One of the kids suggested I allow half-credit for all the questions now answered correctly. I like that approach. Accountability, yet improvement.

One of the kids wanted the room painted pink instead of the drab off-whiteness. It would promote imagination. Okay. The student and I both dismissed the idea as just a joke, but I wonder what effect it would have on the class if they actually did get to repaint the room in a color they chose.

Today I invited the County Prosecutor and a defense attorney to come to my class as guest speakers. That would be an interesting week. They will each be getting back to me.

The question has come up whether I put enough time in for preparation. (Actually I'm the one who asked it.) I like the fact that I'm not putting in 20-hour days and not worrying about being the perfect teacher. I'm reminding myself of law school, where there were several older students who seemed to put in not nearly as much time, panic, stress, sweat or fear as the rest of us. Yet they did as well or better in class. I'm reminding myself a little of that. If I can't be a good teacher at this pace, I doubt I would be able to keep up a more hectic pace for very long, anyway.

Tuesday, Election Day. We talked about the major and minor issues on the ballot in all my classes. In History, we headed into the chapter on the Constitution. As I started to get into it, by calling on the students responsible for Section One of the chapter, one of the brighter students commented, quite audibly and sarcastically, that this class is, "so imaginative and creative." I wouldn't be telling the truth if I said that didn't hurt, because the goal of the teacher is to be just that, imaginative and creative, and in that student's eyes I wasn't achieving those goals. I was probably influenced by that. The class went on to have a discussion about freedom, or lack thereof, of speech. We had an interesting discussion, which was not out of the book. Anyway, the search for innovation is always on.

I mentioned to my loudest student in my loudest class the prospect of referral to the discipline office as the next step. He calmed down a bit, but not much.

The kids asked me how I was going to vote. I told them. They wanted to know why, and I told them. Some didn't agree, but I was pleased to tell them how I felt, while being careful to point out that they don't need to think the same way as I.

Wednesday. Today was the day after the election — pout and gloat day. I'm glad the election is over. We learned some but seemed to spend a lot of time doing it. There will always be current event issues, but no longer one big side distraction.

In my teen law class, I haven't taken any radical discipline steps yet, though I'm tempted to try something they use in elementary school like writing names of talkers on the board, and sending them to the disciplinarian's office for their second offense. It'd feel like failure to me, but that would help the class. You'd like to have a class that's so interesting and the kids are so involved in the material that discussion of discipline issues would not be necessary.

Last night (election night) I went to the courthouse to hang around with the candidates and observers to watch the returns come in. There were a fair number of attorneys in there, (see, you can use the word "fair" and "attorney" in the same sentence after all) and my mind wandered a bit back to my days as a lawyer. For a second, I caught myself longing for my old schedule. I think that one class is wearing on me a bit. I've got to do something about it. I need to take my own advice, to be their teacher and not just try to be their friend. Additionally, the better students in the class deserve a well-run classroom.

On the plus side, this school has some great people. After school today, I was at the gym handing out basketballs for the open gym time. I needed to correct some papers, so while I was doing that, I also watched the kids — essentially the wrestling team against the girls' basketball team — play a game of b-ball. Several of my students and one teacher were involved. It was totally fun.

Three new students came into my math class today, in mid- semester. I'll talk to the counselor to figure out how to grade them.

Speaking of math, today marked a first. There was this very difficult problem the kids were having trouble with. Well, I hope it was a very difficult problem because I had trouble with it, and in fact, could not figure it out. I offered extra credit (a first for me) to whomever got it. A totally great thing happened. One of the kids who is not an A student figured it out. He was totally excited about it. (So was I!)

I will be meeting with a colleague about teaching ideas to be used in History. He is a veteran. He's also the one we had over for dinner last night, and who told us about his vast travel experience and plans. He has used his vacation time well, and in ways to benefit others in addition to seeing the world.

Thursday night. A turning point today. One of my students in my U.S. History complained directly that she did not get anything out of the class and that she thought it was a waste of time. This was the same one who was sarcastic earlier. Several kids, A students and otherwise, jumped in to my defense saying they liked the class, were learning, and wanted to keep it the same. After class I had a talk with the complaining student, about her frustration with doing the chapter work and my problems with dealing with all ranges of abilities. We had a good talk, and I encouraged her to come up with some alternatives, and I would think about some also. I later talked with a veteran teacher who said that problem is very typical, and there are no solutions I am missing. But he encouraged me to try anything I wanted to. He also said it is common for a teacher to feel bugged when the one or five students complain even though 75 percent of the students like the class. You've got to be aware of "the masses" even if they aren't as vocal.

I decided that instead of having the kids do the normal outlining of the chapter and occasional handout, I'll make a couple changes. I'll still assign the kids sections, but they will work on a section as a team and come up with anything they want regarding how to teach the section: a poster, a poem, a skit, an oral presentation like before, anything. A bigger change is that I'll allow anyone who got a 90 on a chapter test to have the option of skipping the next chapter. The alternative they can choose will be to do an independent project of their choice about the chapter, or something in it, and report to the class what they have done. One consequence is that they will only really get into that portion of the chapter they choose to deal with. The benefit is that they will really get into that. Also, they'll probably read much of the chapter anyway to find out what there is to report on. Also, who cares if they don't get the whole chapter? It is only the editor's view of what is important, anyway. Let them enjoy the part they do. They'll get much more out of it.

My guest speaker in Teen Law canceled for Friday. I plugged in an activity that prepares the kids for the test. That'll be tomorrow. Whether I'm too aloof or what, I don't know, but when I got the news that the speaker wasn't coming the next day, I simply took about ten seconds and figured out what had to be done prior to the test. I had to have a quick fix which would help the class get ready for the test.

Friday. What a packed day. I wrestled just a bit with how to deal with the complaint about the boringness of the history class. I talked with my department head and got the go-ahead for my new, or sort of new plan, and told the kids about it today. Those who earn the right to opt out of a chapter can do anything they want, with three guidelines: First, it has to be fun for them. They earned it, so do something enjoyable. Second, it has to be related to the subject of the chapter they're excused from. Third, it should be about the equivalent amount of work as if they did the normal chapter work and test. They will not take the test. They will be graded on their project, and probably get the grade they got on the prior test. They'll show their work to the class. We'll all benefit. I hope they get into it and really have some fun. I needed to clear this with the librarian, who cleared me to release no more than 5 per class to the library to work on their project.

I really felt good telling them about the changes. It's more like homeschooling, in that it'll be more individualized. Also, they'll hopefully get into their topic of interest deep enough that it'll promote greater understanding of the whole picture. I guess that's my rationalization for it. For the following week when they are "in" the chapter and will take the test, they'll be motivated to get their 90 to get out the next week. I don't mind that. I like that. Yes, I am inventing the wheel along the way.

On another subject, one of my best students was visibly upset just prior to class starting. I quickly wrote a note so she could go to the library and have some semblance of privacy. My point in bringing this up involves my reaction. I was upset and concerned about what the trouble was. I didn't think I had the capability to have those feelings, and was glad to find out otherwise. I later asked a classmate if she knew what the trouble was and found it was a minor, temporary problem. I was greatly relieved. Welcome back to the human race, Steve.

Also of note, which I didn't think of until after class, is that this is the end of the ninth week, the 25 percent mark of the year. I'm anxious to see how the next 25 percent goes with my new method in history class.

✒ 10th Week: Nov. 9th - 13th

A veteran teacher ... talked about how things had changed. The '60s were the toughest. Too many free spirits. Alcohol is the main problem now, as it has been for a long time, he said. I asked him how he runs his social studies classes. Pretty much like I'm doing. Throw in some work through the chapters, some group work, some independent studies, and voila, it's school through the decades.

Tuesday night. I scheduled a test for Teen Law today because our guest speaker recently canceled, causing an open day. At the last minute, I got a call from his office indicating that he could make it, so I put off the test to have him come in.

While he was up front, I sat with the students and got a good view of what it looks and sounds like to be a student. I became aware of two things: First, I've been getting down on myself because I don't hold everyone's attention every second. I noticed our guest didn't do that either, and I apologized to him before and after class about the immaturity of some in the class. He's a veteran, that is, he has guest-taught in high school many times, and he said he hardly noticed, and he didn't seem distracted. I learned it's not my fault that the kids buzz a bit. They're built that way. All I can do is provide an atmosphere where they can do their best. For their own good, I should move about three more of the violators. They will be less distracted, the room will be quieter, and the more mature students will have a better class.

The second thing I noticed, which I already knew but can no longer ignore, is that the other kids are distracted by the distracting kids. I guess that's why we use the word "distracting." It is, and not just to me. I will move a few of them, even though that will knock me off the best-loved list.

I heard some staff may be objecting to my "select" students being in the library doing their reports. I will have to check that with the librarian. I hope a few students aren't ruining this for my three history classes.

We went to McDonald's for dinner with the family. My wife is really convinced I go to work as a teacher each day after hearing the high school kids who work or eat there call out my name from all over the place. It's nice to be involved.

I still have too much paper on an around my desk. I need to get organized and throw away a bunch of stuff. It just keeps coming.

I need to be further ahead in all my subjects. That would make for better, more innovative planning and relieve a lot of pressure. I want each day to be exciting, so the kids will want to be there the next day.

Thursday night. Wednesday was a holiday, the first real day off since we started. We've now gone 25 percent of the year. Today some unusual things happened. I gave an assignment to my History kids regarding definitions of the vocabulary words at the end of the chapter. An amazing thing happened. They all did it, quietly. And it will help them on the test. I guess I'm in my paranoid state, wondering about how I'm being perceived, because I was sure they'd give me some trouble about such a routine assignment. They didn't.

On the same score, in my 5th period teen law class, I re-assigned some seats for people who talk too much. To just read that sentence makes it seem (and it probably should be) uneventful. But I really labored over whether it was the right thing to do. To do that causes a "me against you" perception. Of course, it's not me against them — it's me try to create a better learning opportunity for the talkers and for the more mature kids. I was waiting for mass hostility from those I moved. All I got was, "Where do you want me to sit?" That's all. No reaction. Like me wife said, practically scolding me for being so hesitant to take action, it's like dealing with your kids. Discipline is necessary, and it's harder to be a parent than a buddy. Well, it's harder to be a teacher than a buddy. And that's what I'm there for, and I felt good doing my job today.

I talked to a police officer today about being a guest speaker in the law class. It'll be soon.

This year, I'll be the Sophomore boys' basketball coach. Today we had a team meeting. I welcomed the opportunity to tell the kids about the things I consider important and tried to be inspirational. An attentive group of boys. Even though I've been away from organized ball for 20 years (How did I get so old?) it still seems like yesterday that I was in their shoes. Fortunately my boss, the varsity coach, is very open and easy-going regarding questions and help I will need.

Tonight after a second coaches' meeting I noticed a lot of people in the school parking lot. I went inside and caught the last half of a concert put on by the kids. Some classical, some jazz, some '40s music.

Absolutely fantastic. Some of the students are going to Carnegie Hall during spring break. I talked with my boss, the principal, and we sat together a bit at the concert. He's a great guy, but a boss is a boss, at least for the first year. There is a certain pressure to continue trying to convince him that he made the right choice in hiring me.

Back to the concert. An assignment I hope I can work into my History classes is to have a couple of the guys who did solos tonight (one on sax and one on violin) give some sort of interpretive number dealing with an event in history, such as a battle, a court case or a speech.

Great day today. If there is a lesson for new teachers I've learned, for your benefit, and that of the students, be a teacher — don't try to be a friend. (Boy I say that a lot.) In my law class, I had my first lecture/discussion day since I moved the chatters. It was great. One student didn't want to move and asked what would happen if she refused. I simply told her that she'd go to the discipline office. She went over to her new seat, across the room from her friends, actually tried to talk to them from there, gave up, and was quiet in class. It was great. It was the class I had hoped for. A good discussion, with input from kids about the content, lots of questions and on-point discussion. I was about eight weeks too late doing it, that's all.

I had a good discussion with a veteran teacher, who talked about how things had changed. The '60s were the toughest. Too many free spirits. Alcohol is the main problem now, as it has been for a long time, he said. I asked him how he runs his social studies classes. Pretty much like I'm doing. Throw in some work through the chapters, some group work, some independent studies, and voila, it's school through the decades.

I'm going on a camping trip to a cabin with my son and a church group. I'll be coming back to four classes of tests to correct. I better get it done by Sunday, before school, the start of basketball and the rest of life buries me.

🖉 11th Week: Nov. 16th - 20th

In basketball I made the decision to cut two players. Cutting someone is the worst part of coaching. I accomplished the cuts by having the two kids come to my class during school for a brief chat. There was some crying and moaning, but after they left I got my composure back.

Monday, the first day of basketball practice. This is the first time I've coached, with the exception of my son's soccer team this fall. The kids today were all very well-disciplined, good hustlers and eager to please. It'll be interesting to see who shows up for the second day. I want it to be fun. This will require a huge amount of time away from my family. I'm not sure it'll be worth it.

Today I had my history "independent study" people give their reports. It went well and is about what I hoped for. Some did posters, and those will start to decorate my wall. The kids listened well for the most part. It is interesting to see students who are up front become distracted by noise in the room. Now, if I could figure a way to get the noisy kids to do something from the podium, they'd see and perhaps be more attentive.

In my law class, it was more or less back to normal, which is to say a bit too noisy. One kid is just plain chatty, and it's up to me to do something about it. He doesn't have the wherewithal to be quiet. Do I have the guts to move him, or kick him out? Or what? I try to engage him in what's going on, and he tunes in and out. He's very assertive, but usually he directs his energies at the girls in class.

Tuesday. I started the day with some pressure because I really wasn't prepared for either my history classes (three periods) or my teen law class. So, I got up at 5:30, was at school at 6:00, and outlined a few sections in the history chapter, staying just ahead of the kids. A terrible admission. Early in the year I told the kids I hadn't done this book yet, so I'd be going through it just before them, so I don't feel too bad about that. Making the admission doesn't cut down on the need for planning, though. During classes I assigned the sections to the kids, and told them they could work on the sections together and come up with some innovation. Some are playing *Jeopardy* with a section, or doing a poster, etc. Some will simply recite the section in outline form as before, and that's not all bad.

For Teen Law, I went a bit ahead in the book. We're in criminal procedure. I also copied from the Court Rules book some procedures used, and had that handout. These things I'm doing are in the notebook for next semester, so I feel I'll be better prepared then.

I handed out my first discipline referral today — for something that happened in the girls' bathroom. That may need an explanation.

From the hallway, parts of the bathroom are visible. I heard screaming laughter and I saw a student I know running along a ledge. Not appropriate. I easily could've done nothing about it, but that's the easy way out. I turned her in, and she got in minor trouble. When she came to my class later she didn't hide the fact that she hates my guts for getting her in trouble. Who got her in trouble? Oh well. I think the lesson is that I'm to be the teacher, not the buddy. I want them to appreciate me when they're 26, not just like me when they're 16. The teachers that you look back on with respect are the ones who were fair and tough. Not a whimpy pushover. I hope to be fair and tough.

Yesterday on *Channel One* there was a touching story about a nice girl, an A student, a teacher's pet kind of student, who got AIDS through sex with her boyfriend. It was a gripping, sad story, one that had the undivided attention of the class. Immediately after the segment, the room was quiet. Then, out of the blue, breaking the silence, one girl said, "She has nice nails." So, do you laugh or cry?

In basketball I cut two players to get down to 15. A team is normally 12, but I wanted to give as many as possible a chance. There are potential athletes on the team, and I feel a certain responsibility to the head coach to keep these Sophomores progressing. However, the real name for the team should be the "left-over" Sophomores. Approximately nine Sophomores have been moved up to the Junior Varsity or Varsity, so I have the rest. And it's common knowledge that perhaps, just maybe, one from my team will advance next year. What this boils down to is that this is the last year of organized ball for almost everyone on my team. How should that affect how I proceed? Everybody plays? Play mostly just the best to give them a chance to develop? Eternal questions in coaching.

In class, the girl I sent a referral on came up and asked for a favor, to be excused when she shouldn't be — and I said no. I then said, "Gee, aren't I really being mean to you lately?" And she said something to the effect of, "Are you kidding? No way!" My self-esteem doesn't rest on the opinion of one student, but that made me feel better.

In Teen Law I did two things. I gave them a day off from note taking, and gave them an assignment to pick a crime and present it in a group to the class, in the form of a skit, a video, a poster or whatever. They all loved it, and stayed on task the whole hour. I also told them we would be going to the courthouse for an observation day soon. I think it should be a part of the Teen Law program, but I'll worry about their behavior when it happens.

I talked to another rookie teacher today who was refreshingly honest. He said just what a 15-year veteran told me last year when I was visiting his class. The veteran said, as we were back at his desk about one minute from when the bell would ring, "I have no idea what I'm going to be doing in class right now, other than knowing what chapter we're in." Why do I like hearing that? My fellow rookie said he often feels that way. Me too, though I try to have it ironed out for the whole day at least by the time I go to bed the night before. That's still not terribly prepared, Folks.

Today in history class it finally worked. In 3rd period one group made their section into a *Jeopardy* game. The rest of the students got in teams, and it was great. And some learning actually happened. A different group made a board game out of their section. Very innovative and fun.

Substitute teachers around the school had a bad day today. I heard from some students that in one class, the sub handed out referrals for everyone. I guess the kid's were all being a bit loud, and it got to her. A kid said, "We'll, she can't give us all referral slips." I was told she did. In an unrelated matter, a sub got shoved by a student. I've never heard of or seen any student physically touching a teacher, until this.

The b-ball team is doing fine. We put in one simple play, and of course everyone, including me, messed it up a lot. Also, one kid with weird, punk-style hair is on the team. He's a great athlete but certainly is a non-conformist. I thought I was going to worry about stuff like that. I'm not. I'll worry about team stuff as far as getting along and playing together. That might be hard, because I sense the team members are from different cliques. I think the way I'll handle it is to not even think about it.

✎ 12th Week: Nov. 23rd - 25th

Today I had my debriefing on the evaluation. All went well. My own evaluation at this point is that I need to spend more time preparing. However, I also need to spend more time with my wife, more time with my kids, more time preparing for coaching duties, more time working around the house, and more time working with the special case kids who want and need special help. In other words, there just isn't enough time.

Tuesday night. A few things have happened. Yesterday morning the principal told me he had to do a 90-day evaluation of me in my classroom. I vaguely knew something like that was inevitable. I mentioned that my 3rd period history class is a fairly representative example of what goes on in my room, and he agreed to come in for it. It was a good class, with some innovative things going on. Not perfect, but good. Some kids were putting on skits and games to teach the content of their chapter section. However, one student was in the back corner obviously not participating, and I knew it was part of my job to have everyone involved. I unsuccessfully talked to him about joining in.

The principal observed everything, including me, the time when things started and stopped, the students, the objectives of the lesson, and all the clutter in the room. Also, at the request of one of the presenters, he played a part in their skit. Translation: He's flexible and easy going, which makes my job easier.

I should point out that he pops in quite often informally. I'm convinced his purpose on those visits is to help me and be visible to the students, not to intimidate the poor rookie.

My room. I need to have old boxes removed, and have bookshelves in place. Turn a junky corner into the library corner.

The Sophomore b-ball team is coming around, I guess. It's getting more fun now that I know some of the kids a bit better and we are preparing for an actual schedule. Thanksgiving vacation is coming up. I think I won't have practice during the time off. Many of the kids will be out of town with family, anyway.

One of my students had a birthday today. I agreed to send a couple of kids to Safeway (five minutes away) to get a cake. Well, I didn't actually agree to that. They asked if they could, and I said "No." They then asked if they could go the bathroom. I let them go and didn't take any action when they came back, late, with a cake. The "party" went well, except I'll have several bosses cringing when they read this. You simply do not allow students off campus without permission of higher authority and only then for a legitimate reason. I talked with a veteran about that, and he said it's a no-no, but that he's done it, though we shouldn't. My goal is to tell kids that if something like that can be planned even one day ahead of time, I'll help out with class time and be the all-around cordial host and master of ceremonies. But good luck getting me to allow you off campus during the day anymore. That will have to be arranged with the office.

In the "nice timing" category, during class the birthday girl needed to run a legitimate office errand, and while she was gone, the cake-getters came back. That allowed me to hide the cake in the podium, just before she came back, and work her birthdate into the lesson, whipping the cake out in the last few minutes of class. I don't think that one is in the teaching manuals.

I'm modifying my procedure in History. I'll not assign the section work. Having the kids invent ways to do their section has been more entertaining and innovative than in the first part of the year, but I can see it getting old, and it does use a lot of time. On to Plan C. I'll just have lectures and discussions, questions and worksheets. This should allow us to get through the material much more efficiently. We'll see how it works.

Wednesday. Today, in the 12th week, was the first day I realized that my school schedule had cost me my freedom, because I was required to live according to a bell, and that I don't have freedom of movement. That I have to be somewhere at a time beyond my control. In other words, I'm not self-employed anymore. I was driving downtown during my planning period and constantly checking my watch making sure I was back on time. In fact, I don't think I'm even suppose to leave campus during the day without someone's permission.

Today, several male students came in just before the beginning of a class and asked one of my students to come out to the hall to talk about a fight that apparently took place during lunch. Quite a crowd gathered, and I told my student to get back to class and tried to get the other students to theirs. I wasn't totally successful, but another teacher out in the hall was, and the crowd dispersed. During that period, the kid who was involved was called down to the discipline office. I don't think I'll be seeing him for about three days.

Today is the day before Thanksgiving. I gave tests in four of my five classes. In Teen Law, I had the kids show their posters, or videos, or whatever, of what they did to depict a crime. Their presentations led to some discussion of legal points brought up, was a break from the routine, and I'd give that assignment again.

Basketball practice is heating up as we head toward an actual game. I need to get them to work more on defensive intensity, and we'll see what happens. The first game is in about a week. It's fun to be part of the program.

A few times this week I got up early, got to school before 6:00 to get on the computer to get my tests done. During our four day "vacation" I'll spend at least three hours per day either correcting the papers or getting ready for next week. Part of the program.

✎ 13th Week: Nov. 30th - Dec. 4th

I can't wait until I'm more organized. That could be the subtitle of this book.

Monday after the Thanksgiving holiday. I was getting a sore throat on Wednesday, and after coaching/yelling Wednesday after school, I woke up Thanksgiving with no voice. None. A first for me. I don't know what I would've done if it were a school day, but I would've showed up just to see what happened. I got better Friday, Saturday and Sunday, and feel about fine today. I'm re-plugged with a new cold, however.

In Teen Law, I gave back the tests. One of the more chatty kids got a very bad grade, and he was amazingly silent for the period. I motioned him over to me as the crowd lingered around the door waiting for the bell to ring at the end of class. He sort of wandered over, obviously angry at me for flunking him. He has no sense of accountability, but he will after I talk with him tomorrow. I intend to tell him that he has a nice act going — that it works with the girls, probably works on the streets, but it won't work on me or in the job place, so he better learn some responsibility. I don't know if that's exactly what I'll say, but it sounds nice in rehearsal.

You know it's a Monday morning when before first period, there's blood on the hallway floor. Again, I didn't hear a thing. The fight was down the hall about two doors from me. Monday turns out to be payback day for what people didn't like happening over the weekend.

Basketball is getting more focused. The first game is coming up in three days. We're not ready, but big deal. I just hope we can put our pants on straight and get the ball down the court.

Homework. No one in my classes is expected to do much of it, and that may be a problem. No pride in what they've done, because they really haven't done anything other than the daily grind in class.

I got my formal evaluation back. All is well and glowing, as I assume it is with most teachers. I'll try to live up to the principal's kind words. We have a very supportive staff and administration, and I'm fortunate to work here.

So I'm walking down the hall and one of my students stops me — a male student I should point out — and asks me if I want to see something weird. Now, you've got to realize that the setting for this conversation is the 400 hall of my school, a hall I've dubbed the Ho Chi Minh Trail. You'll make it through, but you'll see some blood, hear lots of cussing and threats and generally feel like you're an extra walking through the set of *West Side Story*. So when one of the students who frequents there asks me if I want to see something that even *he* acknowledges is weird, I'm on the alert and my defenses are getting cued. Before I could protest, he started pulling his shirt up and, well, I've seen earrings, nose rings, cheek rings, and oh yes, finger rings, but this is my first sighting of a nipple ring. By the time this book comes out they will be standard attire.

The hall is not that bad. I'm sure in some schools there is actual fear of assault. We just have noisy kids.

Today in Teen Law, the student who was upset with me came up and offered, well it wasn't an apology, but it was an acknowledgment on his part that he has to take better notes and pay attention. When the noise level got high today he even helped get the class back on track.

We started a new unit in Law today, and I'm not as prepared for it as I wish I were. Time, time, time. Also, I've promised a trip to the courthouse. I've got to get that arranged.

Basketball practice is going worse. We were better a week ago. The final practice before our first game is tomorrow. We have a round-robin jamboree, where we, the Sophomore team, play two abbreviated games against the varsity of two smaller schools.

History was odd today. I'm basically lecturing, with some discussion about issues we're studying that can be applied today. In 1st period, no one is awake, which makes it hard to have lively discussions about great social issues. It's pretty bland with me up there talking and trying to draw out conversation. 3rd and 6th period are totally different classes — smaller, livelier, and frankly, more fun. I need to get that energy infused into first period. Having more side topics lined up ahead of time instead of speaking off the cuff (or jotting down notes a day before the topic is covered) will be better. I can't wait until I'm more organized. That could be the subtitle of this book.

I find lately that I'm the first one in the parking lot most mornings. Probably more out of panic and unpreparedness than anything else.

Yesterday I gave my bosses my version of what the class descriptions should be for Teen Law and Advanced Teen Law. My goal in doing so was to have them make one change — to keep Freshmen out. It isn't an issue of classroom management, but one of the effect on the content itself. With the younger kids in there, it affects and, I think, chills the discussions regarding sex crimes, divorce, and other things. I have the support of my department head on this, and we'll see what happens.

In Teen Law I had a detective as a guest speaker. He held the kids' attention, and it was a good hour. He deals mostly with child abuse cases, and a discussion about that will grab anyone's attention.

Last night was the basketball jamboree. I discovered that the Freshmen girls' team was going, but without their coach. He teaches in the nearby town where we would be playing, so he'd just meet them at the gym. Guess who wins Chaperone De Jour award? I don't blame the girls' coach, however, because it would've been senseless for him to drive to town only to get on the bus and head back out again.

This journal isn't about sports details, but at the jamboree, suffice it to say we took second in each "game." We played well early on — and even though we were outmatched, we gave a decent effort. I freely subbed, which cost us some continuity (and points!). A pleasant surprise was that a number of parents were there. I know because on the way to the game, the bus was full with 14 guys on our team and about 12 for the girls' team. We came back with five of our team on the bus and about six girls. Good parent-turnout for a game that was about a half hour out of town.

At the jamboree, one of the other coaches told me that he also interviewed for the job that I got and was a finalist. He's lived in town many years, taught for about ten years, has been head coach of the smaller, neighboring town basketball team for six years, and is a personable guy. I was intimidated by that, and immediately felt a little less adequate for the job. Why'd they hire me?

The initial answer is because of my law background. I realize that I need to work on all areas of my teaching, and be more prepared all the time. I'm not going to suffocate myself with doubt or worry, but I can use events like that to remind me of the great opportunity to help people I've been given in this job. That's why the detective is what he is, and that's why many others are what they are. That's why I am here, so I need to keep pursuing that goal. The only way you coast is down hill.

We have a real game tonight, at home. I see a major issue to be decided is whether I play to win or to give everyone playing time. I suppose that's a question which needs addressing with all of youth sports. I'll specifically talk with the varsity coach on that today. I would like to see us have a fifth quarter, so some of the "better" kids could play more in the game, yet still give the others a chance.

I went to a Fellowship of Christian Athletes meeting yesterday morning. I enjoy seeing the kids in that setting. I also found a great student who lives in our area who wants to babysit. Bingo. I need to take my wife on dates, and finding a babysitter we can trust is a big step.

In History I told about the trip around the country my wife and I took ten years ago. We took two months and a van and camped our way around, with a few stops at friends, relatives and motels. Anyway, the topic we were on had something to do with New Orleans, so I told them about an adventure we had there. The kids loved it. If I have a point to this it would be that I think a teacher who has traveled has a built-in advantage. Not only do you have a better knowledge base to draw from, but having personal stories to share in class is a great teaching tool. Anyway, the story was a good break from the routine, we learned a bit about the area, and a good time was had by all.

One student is having some family problems and came to me for help. I didn't do much, but was there for encouragement, and that made my day. In my student teaching that happened some also. You tend to remember those things more than any content accomplishments.

I can't believe Christmas vacation is coming up. It'll be two weeks of no classes, but not time off completely. I'll have some coaching and be involved in preparing for the rest of the semester. The semester ends at the end of January. My guess now is that I won't use the time very efficiently, but my other guess is that it's healthy to take a break from the action.

I need to write to a few sources for law books for our library and/or my room. How long will it be before I get to that? It's not my "job" to get those, but I discussed this with my department head and the librarian, and since I may be able to get some stuff free, I was urged to pursue it. On second thought, it's probably everyone's job to be on the lookout for good material.

During lunch, another teacher and I needed to make an emergency walk-around in an area of campus kids were rushing to like a herd. That means a fight. Nothing happened, but I think that was because they saw us coming.

Saturday morning. Last night we played in the auxiliary gym while the JVs played in the main gym before the varsity game. After talking with the head coach and getting the pulse of the kids, it became clear that I wanted to conduct the game to win, yet try to do so shuffling kids in and out so all could play. We won the game after making some adjustments at half-time. The kids got the victory and I felt like I did some coaching. One kid did not get to play, so he'll play in the game tonight more than just nominally. I'll start two different people than last night, partly because one kid earned it and because I want everyone possible to experience the honor of being a starter. I also hope to be an active substituter.

After the game, I was on cloud nine. I admit to giving in totally to boyish reactions — to the atmosphere of game night, to the attention the coach gets, to the excitement of the game, and yes, to the win. It was fun getting congratulated by the athletic director, the principal and vice principals, and the other coaches. I hope I didn't strut around too much.

I had my two older kids with me, and after the game we were sitting near the athletic director eating hot dogs, waiting to watch the varsity game. He commented that that must be a sweet moment after the first win, and that the dogs always taste best after a win. It was a filet mignon of hot dogs.

In hindsight it seems silly to react like that, especially since this is "only" the Sophomores, but I would remind any coaches reading this to reflect back on their first win. It was fun being part of the "fraternity" of the school in this new context. The next game is tonight, and we'll see how long this bubble lasts.

Yesterday in school it was a bit of a break day. I lectured /questioned in my three history classes, the math class did their assignment, and the teen law class was given a newspaper assignment. I just learned something huge. In describing the day, I called it a break day. But now I notice the only thing different was that there was a break in just one class, the teen law class. That's my stress class this semester. I hear everyone has one.

I was told by my department head that my idea of keeping Freshmen out of Teen Law was accepted by administration. I think that's a huge piece of good news, and in the not-too-long run will prove to be a greater positive than a basketball victory.

The second grading period was up yesterday, and grades are due Monday morning. I'll spend about four hours this weekend updating my computer disk and entering grades on the school's grade sheet. The computer helps, but keeping up to date on it almost daily would be better.

Now to Saturday night's game. We lost by three after trailing most of the way by about ten. We didn't play well, and the feeling was totally different. In jest, after the game, one of the administrators gave me a thumbs down sign and a dirty look. At that moment it took some effort to know that it was in jest.

✎ 14th Week: Dec. 7th - 11th

Life is full of accountability, and I should strive to require it in this training ground.

On Sunday, the day before grades were due, I spent a couple hours doing the grades. The computer helps immensely, especially in Math, where there are about 45 assignments ledgered. I got them done, and it'll pay to stay on top of them and keep an updated printout. I try to post grades regularly, so the kids can see where they need to do better.

Monday was a game day. School was regular, with me plodding through History, the kids doing their math assignment, and some plodding in Teen Law, although the kids joined in the discussion more than they have. I went home at lunch for the first time this year. I needed to spend some time with my family and take my wife a gift. The reason I did it then is because of the away game tonight.

After school, the team gathered at the gym and eventually took the one-hour bus ride to the game. We lost by seven after being ahead most of the way by a few. We have no offense and have to work on that. During the preliminary game, the kids were not real polite at times, making muffled catcalls regarding girls and refs. You can't take 'em anywhere.

Tuesday. I realized I'll be giving a history test tomorrow, so I had to use my prep and lunch to create and copy the test. I'm glad I didn't wait until tonight to do it. Then I'd have to chance having a copier available first thing in the morning. It's done, which is a relief. This was my first week of just having me do the lecturing and/or leading the discussion, and class went faster. I think as an experiment, I'll do no lecture on the next chapter, just have the kids do work projects in class, and give a regular test. They will be told to read the material and be ready, on their own, for a test. I will be monitoring and assisting on an individual basis.

Wednesday. I couldn't write last night. We had another basketball game in a small town about an hour away, so I got home late. We lost to that school's varsity boy's team. We weren't suppose to do real well, and we didn't. However, after being way down early on, we came back and played them evenly for the second half.

There is a camaraderie developing as I hang around the gym more and am part of the program. I look forward to being there. As a matter of fact, I had 15 minutes before school today, so I wandered up to the coaches' locker to hang around with whomever might be there. It's starting to feel like home. I suppose a veteran on the other end of the career would say it starts to feel like jail.

I started the change today in history classes. The kids are going to read through the chapter themselves, do daily hand-ins, and take the test. I don't think this is plan D, just a time-out from my leading them in discussions and lectures.

I have another cold that is clogging me. I think I'm using that as an excuse to not talk so much in class for a day or two. The real reason is that I just want to try some variety. I realized today a possible side benefit. If the kids don't do as well on the tests without my leading a lecture/discussion, maybe they'll appreciate the information and the discussions more. Actually, the kids in the history classes have been paying good attention, and those are good classes, so I have nothing to complain about.

Next week is the last week before Christmas break, or as it's now called, winter break. Thursday I will give a chapter test in History, and Friday will be, for lack of a better word, party day. We're arranging period-by-period what to do, at least the three history classes, where the kids are responsive and would appreciate something like that. I checked with my department head about that and he indicated usually rookie teachers try a party-type day before Christmas vacation, but most veterans have a regular, busy work day. He said I'd find out why.

I didn't feel well coming home from basketball practice tonight. I was thinking there is no way I could call in sick. There is not one ounce of nobility in that. The plain truth is that I am not organized enough to have a sub come in and have a meaningful day. If I did call in sick, I'd hustle the 15-20 minute drive in there to get my room and assignments ready and give the appearance of having on-going pre-paredness. It'd be a little like cleaning the house so it looks nice for the cleaning person.

Saturday. Last night, all the girls' teams won easily, and it makes me wonder a bit about the fact that we are not as successful. We'll keep trying, and I'll keep wrestling with giving the three or four guys who I think have a good shot at making it next year a lot of playing time, versus letting everyone play, and keeping everyone in the program. I suppose the answer lies somewhere in the middle.

In History several kids mentioned that they didn't like that I wasn't lecturing this chapter, and that they don't like being responsible for the material themselves. I'll be showing a movie next week, the first since about the third week of class. This will be the week before Christmas break, so everyone will be a little antsy.

Today, almost the middle of December, was the first day I took my wife on a date since we moved to town in late August. We went to the dump. (Actually, we did. I had to take our full cans and empty them.) Then we came back to town for some shopping and lunch. With four small kids, soccer practices in the fall, basketball in the winter, and not much income, months without getting out can fly by. We've promised to try to get out twice a month. We found a great babysitter, who unfortunately is a Senior, so I assume we'll be losing her. Anyway, she'll be a great help this year. And after the dump, anything will look good.

I don't know if I've made much progress in the area of having the kids perceive me as their teacher rather than their friend. I want to make progress in that field, even though it may make me a little less liked. It may make me more respected. I want them to be disciplined, and the only way that will happen is if they are accountable for assignments I give them. Lack of accountability causes more peace but less production. Life is full of accountability, and I should strive to require it in this training ground.

✏ 15th Week: Dec. 14th - 18th

A girl came up to my classroom at the end of school Thursday and asked if I minded if she came into my history class 2nd semester. She had heard that I was a pretty good teacher and wanted in. That easily upstaged the generous 90-day evaluation by the principal, though I realize a student's criteria of what makes a "pretty good teacher" may have more to do with being easy than good.

Tuesday morning. I didn't have "journal time" last night because we had basketball practice late, from 5:00 to 7:30. I was home just in time for dinner, dishes and kid things.

We have an away game today and will be back at about midnight.

This is Christmas week and things are crazy. I'm trying a new thing that I won't do again. The kids are working on this chapter of history by themselves, or at least are supposed to be. Most are not using the class time very well, but the A students are. I want to point that out to the others as an example. I'm going to devise a regular test and just see how they do. Maybe I'll let them take it home to finish it. We will all have learned a lesson that way. The lesson I learned is that I can't pass the buck and have the class turn into an independent study — to allow each to proceed at their speed — and be available to help. I thought trying it this one week would be okay, but I can see that too many are not using the hour well.

Maybe I shouldn't approach the history class in terms of chapters. If I had a better knowledge base, I suppose that would be a more comfortable concept. I'm doing that in my law classes. In fact, I decided yesterday that I'm not even going to use the law text next semester. I hope to get the Bar Review outline, supplement it with actual cases to hand out on a weekly basis or so, and liven class up that way.

I find myself hanging on in Teen Law. The class doesn't want to take notes, and I try to work it so they aren't taking notes much more than half of the time. The ones who need to bring their grade up are not taking notes or participating like they should, even though I'm reminding them both during and after class that the notes, or whatever else goes on in class, are the stuff of the tests.

I've found that some of the kids who aren't able to take notes or concentrate as well as the others are in a special studies skills class and work on those problems one or two periods a day. Several of them have come to me and said that's what they're doing, want some extra help, and are paying better attention as time goes by. But there will be about two flunks out of each class. Otherwise, according to my computer, the average of all test scores in all my classes is about 77.

I've determined that either over "break" at Christmas or some other time soon I'm going to go through my room, box up all the prior teacher's stuff that I don't use, and have it stored somewhere. I'll have more ownership of what's going on, and not feel like a visitor or a probationary teacher. I probably am one, I just don't want to feel like one.

One of my bosses saw me doing this journal, and I told him a bit about it. (Until now, the only one who knew was the principal.) For some reason, we talked about teacher interaction and he mentioned that it was only just recently that teachers started sharing ideas and worksheets, etc. It used to be a totally closed-door situation.

It's Wednesday morning in the teachers' lounge. After school yesterday I tried to get on this word processor, but it was in use and would be for quite a while. I went to a classroom and used the one in there in the midst of a noisy practice for the Knowledge Bowl. I had to get two tests ready, one in Teen Law and one in History. I'm giving the Teen Law test today and the History test on Thursday, but one student mentioned she'd be gone and asked if she could take the test on Wednesday. It took from 2:45 to about 4:15 to create both tests, and I'm not sure if they made sense or not because of the Knowledge Bowl activity going on around me. At 4:16, I hustled up to the gym to get the team on the bus to our away game.

The game. We win ugly. The problem is I didn't play all the kids again. Played 11 out of the 14. That's not terrible unless you're one of the three who didn't play.

On the way back, I thought about my week in school. I think in history I'll make this test a take-home test. More learning will take place, and it'll offset the fact that I didn't lecture on this chapter.

It's Wednesday morning and I haven't seen my own kids since Monday evening. I know some guys work on the road and are away weeks at a time, so two days should be no big deal. But when you're use to daily contact it is a big deal, and probably is for the kids, too.

I showed a lousy film in history yesterday. Not lousy, but not great. One class reaction caused me to make some on-the-spot adjustments to my plan. Thank Heaven for the fast-forward button.

Wednesday evening. I lost my TV remote control between 1st and 2nd periods. I felt pretty sure someone swiped it because that happens around schools, and in real life. Luckily I held my emotions in check and didn't lash out too publicly about it. Good thing, because I found it stuck in one of my notebooks the next hour.

There was a meeting after school regarding a student with some learning problems. Since I'm one of this student's teachers, I was involved as the situation was "staffed." I was impressed by the care put in to this one child and the things that were being done to try to help. It takes an enormous amount of resources to try to make it right for even one kid who needs help. I want to also say that it takes an enormous amount of resources to fix what is broken because of what the parents didn't do, though there are exceptions where things happen which are beyond the parents' control. That's not the rule, however, in my opinion.

At basketball practice tonight, I noticed how well one kid hustles. He will "start" the game tomorrow night. I realize that I may have made some mistakes in assessing who the better players are. I may've been duped by flash and show and not been able to see legitimate, quiet, hard work. I wonder if that type of labeling goes on subconsciously in my classrooms? I'll be on the lookout for that.

It's Wednesday evening, and I'm thinking, I have the test made up for my history classes, Teen Law will be a newspaper assignment I'll make up from tomorrow's paper — there are several articles relating to law in every paper, everyday, so this is not a gamble — and Math will be the next assignment in the book. Other than Teen Law, I'm totally ready to go. I think like that a lot, counting through the periods for the next day or two. As I get better, I hope my litmus test each evening won't merely be, "Am I ready to survive tomorrow?" but will be more like, "Do I have an exciting, varied plan for each class tomorrow, and does it take place in a logical sequence for what I will be doing next week?" And maybe, "Do I have those planned for the month?" Nice goal.

There was a fight in the hall, this time between two girls. The teacher across the hall and I both were in the cafeteria on a between-classes coffee run, and no one broke it up. Lots of kids milling around when we got back. No blood, just a lot of negative excitement.

I talked to the owner of the local video store and landed on a gold mine. He explained that all his videos are free to teachers who will use them in a teaching context. I announced to my classes today that starting January 4th, I will be showing a nine-volume Civil War series during lunch in my room. It'll be interesting to see who shows up.

We had a game last night. We were way behind in the beginning and came back. It was a good win. My wife came with our four sons, but she had to chase our two-year-old who ran out on the court during the game. It was cute, but could have been dangerous. They aren't ready for the gym yet.

Today was the last day of classes before the two-week Christmas holiday. I made what I found out was a typical rookie mistake. I fell in to the vacation atmosphere and assumed not much was expected of anyone — kids or teachers. It was a waste, and I won't do that again. All the teachers (I thought) simply had parties and such, showing videos, etc. I did that, and time really dragged. I talked with one veteran who said he quit doing that long ago, and just treats it as a regular day. I'll do that next year.

I created a problem for myself, but I'm glad I did this one. I took down a sleazy poster from the wall of the coaches' locker room. I didn't have the right to do it, but my feeling is that that has no place in school, and certainly wouldn't be fit for a classroom. Kids go in and out of the coaches' room all the time. If not, it'd be a different story, because it'd be a matter of personal taste, and the coach or coaches who want it up there are entitled to their own art. What I should've done is point out my objections to those who use the room, and asked if I could take it down. I didn't do that. I just got fed up and took it down on my own, and that was not correct. We'll see if there's any backlash.

I gave my first take-home test. The kids seemed to appreciate it, otherwise they would've all done terribly, because I didn't "teach" the chapter. That closes an experiment that, at this point anyway, seems like a failure. That's okay. You try and learn by successes and failures.

I got a couple Christmas cards from students, and that felt good. Everyone likes approval. Merry Christmas.

79

✏ Christmas Vacation

I'm reminded of all the problems our society has and how, if done right, the schools could be effective instruments for progress ...

Saturday, December 19th. My first reaction to being on vacation is that I don't really look forward to it as relief from an unbearable situation. My plan for the vacation is to spend time with my family and get some reading done. Also, I've got some tests to correct and would like to get all old assignments ledgered. I doubt I will.

I got talked into (it wasn't hard) entering the teachers' football pool on all the bowl games. As the gambling comic said, "I hope I break even. I could use the money."

Sunday night before school. During vacation, some friends came to visit and stayed with us a day or so. We all got the 24-hour flu. An odd reaction was that I'm glad I got it during vacation. Huh? I think it's harder work to prepare for a sub and to get back up to speed after an absence than to just be there in the first place.

I contacted Bar Review Associates about getting free bar review outlines for my law class. Bingo. They were just in the process of moving offices and had them boxed ready to be thrown out. They sell for about $180.00 each, and I got 96 of them. Free. They are only one year old, which isn't bad compared to the 13-year-old statute books we have now. One veteran asked if they are too advanced for the kids, and whether this is really going to be more useful for me, not them. Answer — it'll be useful for me, therefore helpful for the kids. I'll use the material in a slow and applicational way that is relevant for them.

I visited a university bookstore and picked up some good books on education. I wanted to see if there were any journals similar to this one. There are not, and I guess that's good. I bought a few books about education generally, and started one which is making me think about taking my responsibility to the kids more seriously. After hanging around a big-city bookstore for a while and browsing through some of the education material, I'm reminded of all the problems our society has and how, if done right, the schools could be effective instruments for progress. It is a great opportunity to be a teacher.

Public school is generally at its worst when it is non-participatory, when kids sit in a class as the audience ... I should make my classes more participatory.

Monday, the first day back after vacation. I was apprehensive facing class again. It is very snowy, and the kids are all antsy. The kids tried to tell me that not much is suppose to get done the first day back, but I didn't buy it. Memories of the wasted day before vacation are too fresh. It felt good to get the first period done, and to be back in the swing of things.

In History, I'm lecturing on a couple of chapters that we're basically going to skim through in order to get to the Civil War. The kids got down to business when I did. I also used a different text for "story time" in order to tell another version of the Mexican-American War.

Again, 1st period was quiet and sleepy, and 3rd period was lively and talkative. We had a great discussion about our invasion and conquest of Native American lands, which led to a discussion of different cultural views of the whole concept of property ownership versus simply co-existing with the land. What if we didn't have property rights but could roam around and use whatever land we wished? What would that result in? Most focused on the probable lawlessness, anarchy, chaos and violence because of our greedy nature. Good discussion.

I told the kids who did well and want to opt out of the next chapter that they will have to do more for their independent report than they have been doing. That was understood by all. I think I'll refine that to require that they do something from each section of the chapter (the section review questions?) so they'll at least get the flavor of the chapter they're missing.

In the law class, I told them we'd be abandoning the text book in favor of the Bar Review materials I'd discovered. There was a collective sigh of relief. We had a discussion on the death penalty, because that night a man in our state was scheduled to be executed (by hanging) for killing three children. There was almost unanimous support for the death penalty in the class.

6th period was different. This evening our school has basketball games against Australian teams touring the West Coast. They have a high school varsity and junior varsity team. I spotted the Australian teams in the hall during lunch, cornered about six players, and invited them to my class. We had a good talk about life in Australia. It was certainly not part of the routine, and the class liked it. It took most of the hour, partly — make that probably — because the kids knew that as soon as our guests left, we'd be getting down to other business. Actually, I would have been happy to have them stay the whole hour, but I ran out of questions and discussion after about 40 minutes.

Probably more significantly was that before class, one student gave me a calendar she had received from a congressman over vacation. On each date of the year, it has some significant historical event. The meaningful part was that the congressman told her to give it to "her history teacher." It took about half a day but it finally sunk in. We all have studied history, and most can remember who their history teacher was. I can still see mine sitting at his desk in the front of the room practicing casting his fishing line out the window during class. What finally hit me is, I AM THESE KIDS' HISTORY TEACHER! ME. Now that brings up several points. It brings about a shift in my thinking from being concerned about me, and whether I'll make it through this first year, to wanting to look at my classes from the kids' perspective. What are they getting out of this? Also, what will they remember me for? The responsibility hit hard, and good.

In History, when I read a story from a different book, I was doing so remembering the suggestion from the first faculty meeting, "Go ahead and try it." I think in education we shouldn't hesitate to try new things out of fear of failure, because our education system is in dire need of innovation. Perhaps not trying the new things is failure. I started reading a book over vacation about home schooling, and why it is good. It is kid-centered, innovative by necessity, and probably just plain more fun. Anything that public school can do to be those three things should be welcomed.

During lunch a veteran teacher/coach congratulated me.

"What for?" I asked.

"For having the guts to take that poster down. It's bothered me for years, and I'm glad someone had enough guts to take it down."

He was referring to the sleazy bikini poster in the coaches' locker room. It felt good getting support from a veteran on this issue.

We then went to the cafeteria where we and a few others, including a maintenance man and a counselor, had a discussion on sex-abuse allegations against teachers. Some would debate whether there's a connection between that issue and the poster or not. I am certain there is. In any case there are two of those cases pending in our school right now. The maintenance man mentioned that his union had received a bulletin from their attorney stating that, under no circumstances, are they to be alone in a room with any student. Abandon your job site if you have to, he was told. It's too easy to be accused, and don't invite an opportunity for questions to be asked.

During lunch I had my first day of "Movies At Lunch" in my room. What I'm really doing, for my own enjoyment and education, is watching the nine-part PBS series on the Civil War. There's no way to devote an adequate amount of class time to it, so lunch is it. Only a couple of students came in today. I'll put an announcement in the school bulletin, and see if more kids want to join us.

My Sophomore team lost the game to the Australian JV team. Before the game, the whole county lost power for 20 minutes. A couple of emergency lights came on, and a few flashlights were handed out to coaches. I lost part of my team because parents who live in outlying areas wanted to get home ahead of the approaching storm, and they assumed the game would be canceled. I don't fault their decision. Some who watched how we played probably thought we assumed it had been canceled, too.

Tuesday morning. It snowed all yesterday, so there was some question about whether we'd have school today. I got up at my usual time, about 5:20, and called the local radio station to find out if there was word yet. So far, no cancellation. I went through my shower-and-get-dressed routine, gingerly tiptoeing around the living room where three of our kids were camping out. (We are having a furnace system put in and the basement, where their bedrooms are, is a cold mess)

I drove through new snow on old ice to get to school early to prepare for 1st period. After I was about five minutes from home, the radio announces that schools are closed for the day. About-face, and back to bed for a bit. A free day, and even though I had tomorrow's classes to get ready for, some serious sledding hills were calling.

Wednesday evening. What the student told me on Monday about being her history teacher sunk in a little further. Thinking of it like that caused me to enjoy the day, wanting to be on the "offensive" and provide better things for the students. I'm hopefully going from anxious to eager, from apprehensive to aggressive. I guess in basketball terms it would be a bit like the best defense is a good offense.

I gave a take-home test the day before vacation. There are many kids who have forgotten to bring theirs back. I guess I needed to explain this was merely a take-home test, not a stay-home test. I also need to have a consistent method of downgrading the late arrivals. Naturally, I should have had that all anticipated and announced ahead of time.

With some success, today I called on people to answer or contribute, rather than wait for them to volunteer. I've been doing that a bit, but a veteran suggested it as a way to get the class to stay tuned in. If they know they may be on the spot any second, they tend to stay more involved. He is right.

Thursday. Kids have come up to me lately and asked why they're flunking. I've taken each one over to the computer printout, and have gone through their grades with them. One student had several grades in the 40's (out of 100) and suddenly seemed to understand all too well why the flunking grade. It makes me realize that I've got to get the grades updated and posted for all my classes soon, so all the kids can see where they are and what they need to do with only three weeks left in the semester. I also need to have a consistent plan ready for what the kids who are flunking can do to make up some work or re-take some tests in order to get up to a 60 average, which is passing.

I showed a movie in History today for part of the period. When I previewed the movie I found the first 15 minutes were fine, then it got tedious. So 3rd period, we started off with a discussion regarding whether the Constitution should be amended or rewritten or even touched. The kids knew there was a 30-minute movie waiting for them, so when we were down to 20 minutes to go in the class, they asked about it. I announced with some odd pride that the discussion we were having was better than the movie. And it was. But we did show 15 minutes of it. In 6th period, we never did get around to the movie.

The same three kids are showing up for the Civil War series I'm showing during lunch. I don't know what to think about such a small interest, except that it's during lunch, these are high school kids, and they've got other things going on. I probably wouldn't have gone to it when I was in high school. Anyway, I'm glad I'm showing it. I'm learning a lot.

The weekend. I heard a message in a small study at church which hit home regarding education. The point was that prior to about 400

A.D., the church didn't have a few things which the modern church now takes for granted, such as a building and a pastor. They simply met in homes in small groups. According to a local pastor, King Constantine made these changes because he wanted the Christian faith to be the official state religion. Therefore, it needed a building, because government had big buildings, and more people would come so it would need a big meeting place. It needed a leader for people to look up to and follow, because government had one. The pastor then explained that the number of true believers dropped dramatically as the numbers of attendees increased. The reason is that church went from being participatory in small groups to what it is today — a few performers with most people simply sitting in the audience.

So, compare that to school. Public school is generally at its worst when it is non-participatory, when kids sit in a class as the audience. I think the church example is very relevant, and another example of why I should make my classes more participatory.

How? Have the kids do stuff in class. Okay, what is in the category of "doing stuff?" Talking, reading, drawing, constructing, walking around, arguing, writing. Is listening? I don't think so. So, have them *do* something, and have it be something that they can relate to their current existence, so it'll mean something to them, and they will want to do it. If I can hit one out of those two half the time, I'll be a world ahead of where I (and most teachers, I suspect) am now.

There's a Varsity game Friday night against the rival team. Some guys in class are talking about a rumble. I didn't report the conversation to the administration. I think it's just tough talk.

Friday. Today we had a good talk regarding compromise. When do we leave an injustice alone and when do we feel compelled to step in and fix it? When is that fix a radical, 100 percent job, and when is it a compromise? A lead-in to the Civil War.

Next week is going to be busy. On Monday I'm coaching a game, and won't be home until the kids are in bed. Tuesday, an away game, and won't be home until late again. Wednesday, same thing with a late home game. I bet that Tuesday or Wednesday I'll drive home during my planning period so I can see my family. It's a good thing I only coach one sport.

85

✏ 17th Week: Jan. 11th - 15th

... An appropriate comparison is that no matter how hard I tried, if I walked into the local hospital and tried to do brain surgery, I would not do a good job. As with everything, your efforts need to be more than just sincere ...

Thursday evening. This has been the busiest, and possibly the most meaningful week of the year.

As I was in class today, I realized I hadn't seen my own kids since Sunday night. Basketball games Monday, Tuesday and Wednesday nights meant I got home at about 11:00 each evening, and I leave in the morning before they get up. Throw in a broken-down truck, a tow, a late-night ride home from a friend and you've got a busy week. Oh, and teaching.

Monday in my 1st period class I wrote what I perceived was going to be the schedule for my history classes for the week. It went like this:

    Today - Section 3
    Tues -   Section 4
    Wed -   Section 5
    Thurs - Test

I used the overhead projector, and after I wrote that, I just stared at it for a moment. And a moment longer. The class was wondering what I was doing. It hit me like a brick.

This first period class is my quiet class, with my biggest (at least my most vocal) critic. All year I've been trying to draw them out, but not very hard because I was blaming their apathy on the fact that it's hard to talk about social issues and get riled up at 7:45 in the morning.

Anyway, as I stared at the overhead, as the class wondered what I was doing, a modified plan for the day just popped in my head. I drew the silence out a bit more until all were aware that something was happening, or rather, not happening.

I asked them what that schedule reminded them of. I got the responses I was thinking of, such as, routine, boring, predictable. We came to the conclusion that what it looked like was "school." And we didn't need to do that to each other.

The impetus for the discussion is probably from the book I'm reading which is by, like me, a public school teacher who is home-schooling his kids. The emphasis of the book is that home-schooling works, and it has a lot to offer. Since I am a public teacher who homeschools I am interested in that issue. Actually my wife does the homeschooling. I am, to my shame, mostly just an observer and a shoulder to lean on.

One point I wanted to make with my class was that education shouldn't be like it is in public school, and schools should draw on the good parts of homeschooling or other alternatives wherever possible. This was born out by my students' responses when I asked them to define "school." The words used were words like "boring," "a waste," "dull," "mindless," "hell," "confining," "stress," "costly," "stupid," and finally, to summarize it all up, "a prison."

The way it's done, I don't disagree with their labels. Taking off from there, I discussed about homeschooling, which allows for flexibility and individuality. Interests can be pursued. Bells don't go off every 55 minutes to tell you to quit thinking about one thing and to move on. (When the bell went off, ending the discussion, my critic commented, "Time to go to cellblock C!")

We also discussed my desire to put more innovation in the class and into the atmosphere itself. Anything to liven up this first period. Though not very cerebral, the class decided it'd be a good idea to have a hot water pot going in the morning and, a couple times a week, take a collection to have someone bring in treats. I like those ideas, and got the go-ahead for the hot water. When it comes to treats I don't wait for go aheads, so we were off and running with those surface improvements. I suppose I should be embarrassed writing about a hot water pot and maple bars, but I am willing to try anything.

I'll be the first to admit those changes are basically meaningless when it comes to making school a more desirable place to be than a prison, but, even if atmosphere is a tiny category, it's better to be good in that category than bad. The real difference will lie in whether or not I provide improved opportunities for learning.

This discussion was also spurred by what I learned over the weekend about the history of the Christian church, which I wrote about a few days back. It used to be that churches were home meetings or other small, interactive group meetings with basically no hierarchy in the way. When buildings and pastors and administration came along, so did increased size and the need for structure, ritual and routine, which were necessary to have order when many people were present.

The church went from "participation" to "observation," and lost its effectiveness and personal involvement. The people, which is what the church was meant to be all about, simply became an audience. The pastor and one or two others, or perhaps a choir, became the participants. The result was a drastic reduction in sincere involvement by the average church attender. No interaction. No accountability.

I see school that same way. When the kids are sitting as an audience, they will be bored. I've not seen a teacher who is constantly a great entertainer, though a few skills in that area would certainly be helpful. But, once the student starts doing stuff in class, he'll be more involved, so long as he's accountable.

I also pointed out to the kids that when they go somewhere and spend time doing something to earn money, it's called that four-letter word, *work*. And they'll have to do it, like it or not, treats or not. I pointed out that we will have to be spending a substantial amount of time on the first Bloom's levels of knowledge and comprehension before we can go on. I admit I stuck that in the discussion to relieve me from having to be Mr. Innovation every day.

After Monday's discussion and collective sigh of relief, we all felt we were about to turn a corner. But I felt the deserved, self-inflicted pressure to make a few changes. During the week, by the way, we were on the chapter dealing with the events directly before the Civil War. I came up with a few things the kids could do for half a period, and I held a lecture/discussion the other half. It was much better than lecturing to them the whole hour.

This morning I intercepted a fight about to happen. It's amazing how the crowd gathering is easy to spot. I knew one of the boys involved and I will have a talk with him about life priorities, options and problem-solving skills.

I heard through the grapevine a compliment about how I'm doing this year. At least at the survival level. That felt good, because it wasn't someone saying something nice to my face just to be socially correct.

A good starting point is the relationship with the kids. The next step, moving on to actually being a good teacher, is something else, and it takes work that I'm just beginning to see. An appropriate comparison is that no matter how hard I tried, if I walked into the local hospital and tried to do brain surgery, I would not do a good job. As with everything, your efforts need to be more than just sincere, they need to be done with knowledge of how to carry out those good intentions. I feel this week I've turned the corner a bit in realizing that.

I talked with a student who wants to be a high school teacher and to be involved in changing education so that students have freedom to learn. It was a nice talk, but what she wants is what everyone wants, and the only way to accomplish that is to reduce the teacher/student ratio to about 1:10 and eliminate classes as we know them. I support that, but it's not what is or will be in the near future at public school.

Friday. I gave tests in the three history classes, and that gave me time to prepare for next week's classes. I don't give multiple-choice tests exclusively, so I will be spending a substantial amount of time this weekend correcting three periods worth of tests which are about one-half essay. I feel good about the breadth of information tested on and the varying Bloom's levels used.

Between 5th and 6th period, a magazine ad for baldness prevention mysteriously appeared on my podium. Cute. My hair loss has been a running source of humor and mock depression all year.

The end of basketball season is coming, and I'm looking forward to the time to prepare for classes better than I have. To have more things for the kids to do, not just to listen to.

In the coaches' locker room the topic came up about how teaching and coaching compares to lawyering and judging. We discussed that coaching is a pressure release, and is way more fun than I thought it would be. Being a first year teacher is pressure-packed, they all agreed. The type of pressure, however, is way different than lawyering or judging. In the classroom, no one's life or custody of their child or a large hunk of money is directly hanging in the balance if you screw up. The stress, though constant, is way less. Also, in law your personality is affected because you have to develop pretty tough skin and remain aloof from the problems you deal with. I suppose the same could be said about teaching, but I haven't seen that yet in my experience. In fact, one of the reasons people give for being in teaching is to help the kids. That requires involvement.

Another kid I know was almost involved in a fight today, and I took him aside to give him a "maturity speech." I have no idea if any of it will stick.

✒ 18th Week: Jan. 19th - 22nd

So there it was, a little microcosm of the problems of society, right there in my classroom in living, bleeding color ...

Tuesday night. In History, I'm in the Civil War and for reasons I touched on last week, I don't feel like just going through the chapter lecturing. I reviewed a few other sources, and got some good quotes and stories about the war. Today in class I did that and it went okay. I emphasized that I'm not a military strategy guy and will spend almost no time on that aspect. I'm more interested in why the war happened, how people were affected, and the things it caused as a lead-in to the next section I'll be teaching. I was at the school at about 5:30 this morning making sure of my lesson plan and getting some grades on the computer. That's not planning, that's panicking. However, a nice controlled panic does seem to get things done.

Tomorrow I plan to hold a funeral for the Civil War dead. This will be with lights off, a candle burning, and with the death statistics slowly revealed on the overhead. If I notched up one death per second, it would last for almost eight days.

About a week from today is the last of the semester. I'm getting my grades updated on the computer for at least two reasons: So the kids will see what's missing or incorrect so they can correct it, and so that I'll be caught up and all I'll have to do is put in the final test grade. Tests are Tuesday and Wednesday, and I think grades are due the following Monday.

My truck lost its transmission for the second time in five days. It's in the shop, fixed, but I need to leave our van home because my wife is taking the kids somewhere. I called to arrange to take the school bus tomorrow. Our school secretary and the transportation guy laughed when I said what I wanted to do, but that it would be fine. So tomorrow at 6:45 I get on a bus with Kindergartners and Seniors and everyone in between. And it'll be my birthday. Happy 41st.

In Teen Law I'm arranging our field trip to the courthouse this Friday. I got the form turned in, so now it'll just be a matter of getting the kids where they're supposed to be at the right time, and not losing them at the courthouse.

I finally got the hot water (for coffee, tea or hot chocolate) for my classroom. I asked the morning janitor to plug it in about 6:00 so it's ready by first period. I will normally be doing that, but tomorrow I'll be squirming around on a bus with some second graders, thank you. Someone has a doughnut run financed, so it should be a pleasant start to the funeral for the Civil War casualties.

The hot water pot, however, doesn't make me a better teacher, and I still need innovation for that. A constant struggle, agreed a veteran today after a faculty meeting.

At the meeting, about the only thing discussed was the fact that a sexual misconduct case is a time-consuming struggle. Our principal explained that's why he's not as visible around school as he'd like to be. Also, funding is needed for a new elementary school. The elementary school principal came and gave a pitch for why we need to get the public out to vote for funding for the new school.

I can't find one student's old test, and she insists she took it. My attendance record indicates she was here on test day. My fault, and I need a good solution. This reminds me of the P.E. teacher who lost his grade book near the end of the semester. His solution: If he didn't know the kid, he gave him a B. If he did know him, either because he was earning an A, or was a problem, the teacher graded accordingly.

Wednesday. This morning I got to school on the bus. When it came, the first thing I had to do was make sure my dog went back to the house. She dutifully followed me out our driveway and down the lane to the main road. I might as well have been a kindergartner on the first day of class. The dog dropped her head and sadly walked back home, and I got on the bus with the kids. It was uneventful, and I was surprised how well-behaved the kids were. We were listening to the scanner, and kids were commenting how lousy all the drivers are based on all the accidents that were getting reported. I should point out it was a snowy, slippery morning.

The funeral. Lights were out, curtains drawn, their attention was mine, at least for a few seconds. I got the match lit, the candle lit, and placed it on the podium. In one of those quirk deals, though, I was trying to set a somber mood for a funeral, but some of the kids had heard that today is my birthday and thought I was having a party. After I put that down, the mood was set, and we had a meaningful, and I actually think, memorable, discussion about death in the Civil War, and in war generally.

We lost a basketball game to a bigger and older team. I lost my temper for the first time in ten years. I yelled a bit and kicked a garbage can. It had nothing to do with the game, but with what I perceived as a careless attitude by some of the kids following the game. I learned that losing my temper didn't solve anything, but I sure got the kids' attention.

In Teen Law, my wild class, I commented that we only have a few days left, so let's all hang in there. My temptation is to give them some sort of speech about discipline and accountability. I suppose I somewhat blew it by allowing re-takes on tests, etc. and the real lesson on accountability could have been learned by some of them not passing. I have held a few hands to get them through.

Thursday night. Today at lunch I was watching the Civil War movie in my class. A kid opened the door and asked a kid in my room to come out to the hall. He did. I heard some noise and then about five seconds later, the door swings open and the first kid was attacking the kid who had gone out from the room. This is my first "at the scene" fight and there wasn't much time for thinking, so I sort of jumped up and waded around the kid who was getting hit and slid into the assailant, yelling at him to knock it off and moving him back. The victim stayed back in my room, bleeding pretty good all over the floor while his face was swelling. I called the office for help. It appeared like the victim would need medical help, but it turned out not on an emergency basis. One student stayed in the room with him and gave him a box of Kleenex, all of which was blood-soaked within seconds. The kid was really bleeding. I talked with the assailant for a bit, who freely gave me his name. I confirmed with students standing around that that's who it was. I then divided my time between crowd control in the hall and keeping my next class out of the room so the victim could have some peace for a bit and so the janitor could clean up the blood. By then, now only a few minutes after the assault, the principal and other people who deal with that type of problem had arrived, and all was calmed down.

I had one additional concern. I used a few clean Kleenex to clean up some of the other Kleenex and blood spots off the floor. I have an old cut on my hand, and there is a concern about AIDS whenever you deal with blood. I think I was safe about it, but realize I didn't have any gloves handy. Immediately after school today I got several pair.

Later in the day, I talked with the administration about what would be the sanction for the assailant. Three days for a fight. Five days for an assault. I politely expressed my opinion that kids who pummel other kids ought to be restricted from campus for about six months, pointing out that about 1,380 kids want to be in school, and they shouldn't have to be stopped by the 20 or so who are assailants.

It turns out the assailant has a very full and sad background including drug addiction, being victimized himself, and long-term attempts by his family to solve the problem. So there it was, a little microcosm of the problems of society, right there in my classroom in living, bleeding color.

How will I change, or what will I do in response to this? I told the administration I would be happy to put time in on a committee to review sanctions for discipline problems at the school. I think my Juvenile Court background can't hurt in that regard. I don't have any better answers than the next person, but I do think we need stiffer sanctions than I learned about today. The principal agreed the whole thing needed reviewing.

Back to school. I'm going on the courthouse field trip tomorrow morning for a few hours. That means I've got to get the room and assignments ready for a substitute. Getting ready for a substitute is a good exercise to go through. It made me clean up my desk area, get the day's assignments all organized ahead of time (is 18 hours ahead of time?) and otherwise be prepared to let someone else know how you are doing. In getting ready, I found 5 texts and my old sweater which had slid down behind my back desk.

In History, I've got a map project regarding the battles of the Civil War, which I intentionally did not cover in today's discussion. I fear there will be some comments from some of the advanced students that this is mundane, third grade-type work. That'll be perfect for some of them. Anyway, it will give all of them some involvement with our topic in a hands-on way.

In basketball, I continually get frustrated that I can't have all the kids in the game for long stretches, so they can get into a rhythm. So today I found a partial remedy: I got the scoreboard out, got a coach and a player from the JV/varsity team to ref, and had an intrasquad game. The kids liked doing that, it sort of felt like a game, and I felt better that they all got to play basically the whole game. The Greens vs. The Whites. I need to do that more, though there's only about one week left in this season. Like in the classroom, my kids next year will benefit from the mistakes and omissions I made this year.

Friday. Today was my first solo field trip, taking the teen law class down to the courthouse. Everyone who was supposed to be there was, and they all showed up at the end to get on the bus when it was over. In between we wandered from court to court and saw different things. Much of what goes on in real court is slow, so at times they were bored. However, I was impressed with their — here's an old teacher word — deportment. We should have done that early in the semester. They would then maybe have a better context for their questions during the semester.

The hot water pot in the room has been a mild hit. Kids are storing their mugs in my desk drawer, bringing in their tea, hot chocolate, etc. and otherwise using the privilege very appropriately.

One student asked a question which sort of brings a teacher back to basics. This is a student who is not real involved, but appears to try when he is here. He has lots of disadvantages and problems outside the classroom. Anyway, we're going over the Civil War, and before class ended I wandered back to his corner and chatted with him a bit about an assignment. I discovered he didn't really know what topic we were on, let alone how to do this specific assignment. I opened his text to a map of our country showing the states which seceded from the Union. I gave him about a one-minute capsule of the entire story. Before I finished, after he comprehended what was going on and he was actually getting a little enthused he blurted out, "Who won?"

At least he knew enough to ask an important question.

A review of the last 24 hours: Stopped a fight and helped clean up the blood. Coached one and refereed part of another Sophomore basketball game. Got ready for a substitute. Took a class downtown to the courthouse. Actually spent a few evening hours at home and played Jr. Monopoly with two of my kids. And taught my other classes.

Usually I'm dead tired and go to bed by about 9:30. Occasionally I plan to stay up and talk about something with my wife. The reality is even then I don't comprehend much of anything that happens after about 10:00.

✎ 19th Week: Jan. 25th - 29th

We hear the story that one reason to teach is that you never know how far your influence might carry. You tell something to one student, who teaches it to someone else, etc. That implies something good is being taught. That isn't always the case.

Monday. My first problem with this week is what to call it. I always believed that the semester was 18 weeks long, since the school year is supposedly 36 weeks. This is the 19th week, and we are still in the first semester. Just barely, though, because after today, the rest of the week is devoted to finals, book collection and grading time.

To get ready for this week, I spent about five hours this weekend getting the content outlined for my law and history classes, and writing two tests. I needed to have them ready by today, because tests start Tuesday, and the copy room will be busy with teachers getting prepared. So, I got both tests done by Sunday night and copied one before school today. I found I needed to edit the law test, so I wasn't able to get that one done until my 4th period planning hour.

In classes today, I spent about 40 minutes on new content, and about 15 minutes helping students make sure they were getting old assignments in, and handing out tests which students wanted to re-do under the "one re-take" rule.

With the tests copied and ready to go, this is looking like an easy week. Tuesday is set for two hour finals in periods 1, 3 and 5. Wednesday is finals for periods 2, 4 and 6. I will be sitting for the whole day while my classes take their tests. In reality I will be going over chapter 13 in my history book and getting ready for next week, the start of the second semester.

In 6th period today, we arranged for a pizza party after the final on Wednesday. The kids in that class won't have tests Thursday (the last day of their week), so I figure it's okay.

I'll have the same schedule next semester, and the same kids in my history (1st, 3rd and 6th periods) and math (2nd period) classes. Teen Law is only one semester, so I'll have a new bunch. There are a couple exceptions, especially in the math class where some kids only needed one semester. A couple of the kids who are bowing out are quite, let's say, social, and I can't say I'm sorry to have them out. I vow to have a quieter class next semester regardless of who's in there. I simply intend to clamp down a bit.

I noticed that in math class especially I never really developed a relationship with the class. It is a diversified group, and maybe the nature of the independent work on the material doesn't call for as much interaction as the other classes. I'm not going to kick myself over it, though.

I do look forward to a new shot with a new Teen Law class. That will be different. I intend to approach the content entirely differently, and expect the class to be more disciplined. I'm not going to be using the text book, but rather the Bar Review outline. There will be more use of actual cases. Just plain more preparation on my part will make it a better class.

I discovered my computer grading system has a glitch. I reached 60 entries, and it won't go any higher. I talked with another teacher who had an idea how to get around that limit, and I'll give it a try tomorrow. I'd hate to have to do all the grading by hand at the last minute. Live by the computer, die by the computer.

Maybe it's the light week in front of me, but tonight I seem to be enjoying teaching and prospect of future teaching more than a while ago.

Tuesday night. Today was the first day of finals. I didn't give a comprehensive final in either History or Law, and the kids got through with the chapter final in an hour or less. As expected, they didn't really use the extra hour to study for their other finals, so it was a bit of a waste of time. Some were studying, though. Even as kids are turning in their final exam for the semester, they're still asking if they can do extra credit.

It's amazing the kind of junk that kids read. There's a lot of good writing out there, and I'll add to my list of things I want to accomplish is to influence them to read better books than the pulp violence or sex novels I see them carrying.

I should start an "incredible questions I can't believe they asked" list. Today alone I was asked at least five times if there was a comprehensive final in our history class, after I explained during the last few weeks at least a dozen times that we were just having a chapter test. I know my frustration is founded because as one of the kids asked that, about three other kids from different parts of the room answered the question for me.

I noticed something subtle and good has been happening. More and more the kids are hanging around during the last minute or so before class gets out, chatting with me about everyday stuff . I felt I had a generally good relationship with the kids from the start, but this seems a good sign regarding my past and future effectiveness.

I got to be a hero at basketball practice today. A coach of a different team came over to be part of an end-of-practice contest. My last-second long shot beat the other coach's last-second shot so our side won, and the other side had to run lines. That made my season.

I enjoyed the light day. I reviewed most of the next chapter in history, thinking of innovative things I could do. I need to do the same thing for law class.

I got a call from a friend with a legal problem. I should mention I continually get asked legal questions, and they immediately take me back to my "old" profession. I'm glad to try to help, but I enjoy not dealing with that stuff on a daily basis.

Thursday night. Last night, Wednesday, we had a basketball game. I'm going to talk about this game more than others because even though this journal is not meant to be about coaching, I think some things happened which were among the most intense things of the year, could relate to the classroom, and caused me to think about my performance.

One of the players hasn't been getting the playing time he had earlier in the year. I didn't recognize his dejection until last night. I put him in the game as a substitute, but he was too dejected to play to his potential. I had to take him out after about a minute of play because it was obvious he wasn't mentally ready to play. The tough-coach answer to that is that it's up to the player to "suck it up" and to get tough if things aren't going his way. Play tougher, do better, and earn more playing time.

There are a couple of problems with that for me. I'm not a tough coach. At least not yet. Maybe after another year or so, I'll have thicker skin and simply ignore complaints about playing time. But this is my first time dealing with this and I'm taking it seriously. His parent talked to me and wondered why he was being punished. I said that certainly wasn't the case, it's just that playing time was being allocated on who was performing according to what was asked, and he wasn't doing that. Additionally, he's played at least as much as anyone else. Less playing time results in loss of confidence, which results in a reduced performance, which results in less playing time — and the vicious circle is on.

I have been playing other players more, and that's a good thing. But I do need to review my handling of each player because of the confidence and esteem factors involved in young athletes. Veteran coaches will read this and pass it off as a rookie coach being too sensitive. I'm now living through it as a rookie coach trying to grow from the situation. Perhaps it's bugging me because I sense I did make some mistakes in handling the situation.

I had a private meeting with the player today and attempted to get the situation back on track. The program is here for the kids, and that entails a lot of stuff. I need to keep all the stuff in perspective.

So, how does that relate to the classroom? As a coach, I have enormous — way too much power — over the kids. A coach could jerk their strings around and really play with their emotions. It easily could happen intentionally, and just about as easily could, and does, happen unintentionally. In the classroom, there also could be the chance to affect a kids' motivation, self-esteem and desire to push on in the right direction. I need to keep that in mind about each kid, every day. We hear the story that one reason to teach is that you never know how far your influence might carry. You tell something to one student, who teaches it to someone else, etc. That implies something good is being taught. That isn't always the case.

The season ends in a few days, with our last game coming next Monday night. We'll see how it all goes.

I showed an AIDS movie in class today. It was not well-received, and I only showed it one period. Later I found out that because of its graphic nature, it had been determined inappropriate for our campus and was not to be shown. Oops.

Tonight I'll continue to grade papers, and hopefully get the grading for the semester done tomorrow. My opinion of these test days has shifted. I really have not enjoyed these "light" days of doing desk work while the kids are taking tests. Now I know how end-of-semesters go, and I will be better prepared next time. I should've talked with a veteran more about what to expect. One simple solution I intend to implement is to have a comprehensive final. The kids will know that from the first of the semester, so they will be forced to be more serious about doing their daily work and keeping it organized for review at the end of the semester. Also, the comprehensive test will allow for an additionally walk-through of all the material. Both of those are good. A weaker, but still valid reason for the comprehensive final is that it will also keep them busy for the two hours allocated to each class during finals week.

We had an all-school assembly today with a national sports figure as the key speaker. It turned out to be an exercise demonstration with a product which was not explicitly advertised, but it was mentioned that if you wanted to buy it, contact the speaker. The kids didn't seem to enjoy the presentation and felt that they were being used because of the commercial nature of the show. I agree with the students, and felt the assembly was inappropriate, as did other faculty I talked to.

I need to get my teen law curriculum ready for the start of the next semester on Monday. I'm looking forward to a new start. This will be my first attempt at teaching a class the second time. I don't have a lot of time right now to do a lot of preparing, but I will once the first semester grades are in.

Friday night. No classes today because it was a teacher work-day to get final grades done. I didn't. I learned a valuable lesson. I made the rookie mistake of accepting late and make-up assignments right up through the last day. I spent much of today grading make-up work, and didn't get to the chore of tabulating final grades until around noon.

I talked with veterans about this and the suggestion which makes sense is to have a written policy which states that you'll not accept late work after ten days from the original due date, and even for special cases (there are *always* special cases) will not accept old or make-up work within ten days of the end of the semester. I intend to get the grades done sometime tomorrow. They are due 7:45 Monday morning.

There was a good resolution with the player issue. He had a good practice today, he'll start in our next game, and I look forward to him contributing. Actually, that decision was made easy for me. For other reasons, a couple of the other players weren't at practice, so they won't start. I am relieved tonight that my first player and parent conflict seems to be over, at least for now.

✒ 20th Week: Feb. 1st - 5th

A girl in class was crying over boyfriend problems. I don't know the severity of the problem, but to her it was a big deal. I tried to send her to the counseling office because I don't want sobbing in the room. It's distracting. Like Tom Hanks' line from the women's baseball movie, A League of Their Own, 'Crying? There's no crying in history class!!'"

Monday night. Lots has gone on since last week. I spent about five hours over the weekend getting grades done. For the final grades, I had some extra philosophizing to do, since these counted. Sixty percent was the minimum passing grade, but in a couple instances, I granted a D (there is no such thing as a D- in our system), where the student had at least tried and was within a few points.

Today was the first day of the second semester. It was just as important as the first day back in September, but I had two different reactions: First, it wasn't that big of a deal, and second, I was ready for it. The last few weeks have given me a feeling of confidence and more control. A little less worrying about things that might go wrong.

I'll have one entirely new class, Teen Law. That's the class I was sure was a world record for lack of discipline and, let's say, socially active kids. Today after I was with the new class, I realized I was more right than I thought — 30 kids who don't know each other sat quietly. So quiet it was spooky. I had trouble getting on track because I got a teacher's wish to the extreme: all eyes and ears were on me, intently. Wow. I better have something for these kids because it appears that they may be a bit passive. But I do appreciate their maturity and attention. Maybe I'll actually be able to present lessons and trust them to handle assignments maturely. We'll see.

One of the teachers in our hall was gone today and didn't leave a lesson plan. I am certainly not throwing any stones because I have very little in the way of a plan if I were taken out by a sudden illness. The sub, who is a veteran, was going around asking if any of us had a video available. I didn't, but I did have a worksheet relating to the subject matter. And the only reason I had that is because I had just borrowed it from a different teacher. I need to get about three canned plans in my drawer that would be good for a sub to use any time.

2nd period math class is a bit the same way. Several students only needed one semester of math credit, so the class is smaller by about six or seven people, and that makes a huge difference.

1st period went from about 26 kids up to 34. It felt like a convention in there. There are some talkers and I sense that the 1st period blahs I had last semester won't be as bad this time around.

I'm getting convinced that going from first year into the second year next fall won't be the end of my learning curve. (Note the chuckles from the veterans.) I won't be totally prepared for every moment just because I'll have a notebook full of content and lesson ideas. Well, not full, but at least started. I can see there will be constant adjusting and weeding. From an education standpoint, that's good, but I will look forward to not spending as much time going over the basic content to get myself up to snuff. I find that being over 20 years and two careers ahead of the kids helps to fill in gaps in the lessons as far as applications and connections to things I know they will be facing.

We had our last game tonight. It's amazing in life that one little thing going wrong can affect you even if everything else is right. An hour before the game, out in the hall, there was a scuffle between one of our players and one from the other team. I benched our player who showed what I would call bad judgment. It kind of put a damper on things. Anyway, we won the game in overtime, which was fun, but frankly the victory had nothing to do with my coaching. Our kid happened to make a shot at the end so we look good.

The issue regarding the other player who was seeking more playing time was resolved, with him getting back in the starting line-up and playing well.

Tuesday. I had a discussion with the parent of a student whom I had in two classes fall semester. He is a bright student, but doesn't do much in the way of class work such as, say, be there. Or take notes when he is there. He's very polite though. I told her I flunked him in one class and passed him in the other. She was concerned that he be taught a lesson on accountability. If anything, she thought I was too lenient. I noticed in class today — I have him for one class this semester — he did have his notebook out and was paying attention.

In Teen Law I had my first experience of teaching something for the second time. It was a bit awkward being fresh with something I knew wasn't fresh, but this class appears to be mature, and it went real well.

About five minutes into one of my history classes, a new kid said he hadn't taken this many notes all year. My veteran students sort of looked at him as if to say, "You ain't seen nothing yet," and they're right. I tell students who complain about note taking that it does no good to sit in class and stare blankly or talk with their neighbor under the guise that they'll get the notes from someone later. The act of taking notes requires being involved in ways most students wouldn't be if they could just do seatwork assignments with their buddies. For notes, they have to listen, observe, and convert what they hear and see — I put highlights on the overhead — into their own notes. It requires doing and thinking. And not just about history, but about current applications I attempt to branch off to. If I can keep them doing that, I'm ahead of the game. More importantly, they're ahead of the game.

A veteran coach talked with me after school about the season and congratulated me on a job well done. It felt good getting strokes after a rookie year, even though it was more fun than work, and I know I could've done much better.

I learned two things during this season: You can either keep 15 players or go lie down on the freeway. The result will be the same — you're going to get run over. Never, under any circumstance, keep 15 players on a basketball team. It's not fair to any of them because playing time is so diluted. Now that our school has started an intramural league, the pressure won't be so great to keep every kid who wants to play. Second, never be in or around the gym when they're looking for help setting up for a gymnastics meet. That stuff is heavy. They don't teach you that in your ed. classes.

I have "bus duty" after school this week. I was talking with another teacher about safety problems related to a barrier to keep students back from the curb. He pointed out that a note or petition to someone would bring results in about ten years. It's no one's fault — just a matter of lack of funds. In fact, today there was a school levy in our district to build a new elementary school. It failed.

I had to get re-fingerprinted at the police station today. The fingerprinting is a requirement of the State Superintendent of Public Instruction Office, and I guess my fingers didn't work right the first time. I hope it never matters.

I'm toying with the idea of going to the Junior Prom this weekend to take a bunch of candid (?) pictures of students I know. We'll see.

Wednesday. We had an interesting teen law class. It's still very quiet and attentive, with a little buzzing as the kids get to know each other better. I was lecturing on a topic and telling some war stories and such and all was going well. I glanced at the clock to see how much more time I had to go, expecting I had about a half hour. I had less than 10 minutes. Time flew. I think a characteristic of a new teacher is that you are worried how you can fill the hour, so you hope it flies by. As I teach more, I'm not so worried about that, and more concerned that I get the content out and have good interaction, and let the time just take care of itself.

Math was interesting today. A few more people are getting added, so it's not as small a class as I thought it'd be. Anyway, I was back helping a student at her desk. When I finished I turned to return to the front of the class. The students were asking me to help with a problem, so I went to the overhead and started working on it, with the kids still paying attention. At some point during all that, I noticed my department head standing over by the door. I'm not sure how much he saw, but I was involved with the students, and things were going fine. It's nice to get "caught" in that situation.

I got a wild call today. The campus representative for our local, city-wide teacher's association informed me that I had been nominated for President of the Education Association and wanted to know if I'd be interested. As a rookie, I have no qualifications for that type of job. I don't have any idea what the association does or how it does it. I told our campus representative that, but I'd like to talk to him about the whole thing before deciding. I'm meeting him for lunch tomorrow.

I did a study sheet for my history classes today. It went fine, and they got a break from listening to me lecture for a day.

Thursday. I got to class only a few minutes before the first bell. I was really rushed after the Fellowship of Christian Athletes (FCA) meeting. Once I got to school, I had to speak with the athletic director about a banquet for the basketball team coming up next Wednesday, which will amount to a dessert pot luck with the parents of the Freshman and Sophomore teams. I've got to finish a role of film tomorrow so I can get the pictures I took of the team developed by the time of the banquet.

I had a lecture/discussion in History and Law classes today, and all went fairly well, given the format I've chosen. One person mentioned in 6th period, which is the loosest and most relaxed class, that "this is the oddest class," or words to that effect. She's right, because the kids are ready, willing and able to join in the discussion, and sometimes our discussions take us to odd, though relevant, places.

One student who just got his report card proudly mentioned out of the blue that, "In [another class] I thought I was going to crash and burn, but I got a D." So much for not crashing and burning.

My T.A. for 5th period (Teen Law) is a guy who was in Teen Law last semester. It'll be interesting to talk with him about how the class is different this semester than when he took it.

A T.A. in a different class tried to convince the attendance office she was in my class on a day I know she wasn't. In order to feel confident of that I had to have reliable records. I did in this case.

Teen Law is shaping up. I've actually got a plan, and it seems to be working one week into the semester.

We had a great 6th period history class. The school paper came out today, and two students in the class had editorials in it. After I went through an abbreviated version of my planned lesson, I had them read their letters to the class. One letter dealt with students being immature because of the prejudices which develop if you aren't in the right group or clique. The other dealt with an alleged narrow-minded administration approach to the Junior Prom — you are only allowed to go if you have a date of the opposite sex. In other words, no singles, no buddies, no gays or lesbians. The fact that school reflects issues in society shows again.

This coming Monday and Tuesday, my history classes won't be taking place because the Juniors are going to a career-counseling deal. We just finished a chapter Friday, so the test will be Wednesday. I'll make up the test this weekend, so I'll have Monday, Tuesday and Wednesday of no work in class and will be able to get ahead. I know I'm going to skip some chapters soon so we can get up to the 1980s by the end of the semester. I find I'm reviewing three sources now: our text, a simpler and more general text which I like better than ours, and *Don't Know Much About History* by Kenneth C. Davis. I occasionally have "story time" and read anecdotes out of the latter to the class.

I'm trying to get ready for the dessert banquet next Wednesday for the basketball team. I'll be presenting each player with a certificate, an anecdote, and some kind words. It should be fun, but I know there are many parents who think their son should've played more. Next year, I won't keep 15 players. Maybe six.

✐21st Week: Feb. 8th - 12th

Last night I was at Safeway and talked with one of my students who is a bagger there. He works there part time and at another place, for a total of about 40 hours a week. This in addition to school. And he's not the only kid like that. Knowing there are many such kids in that situation affects my expectations at school. Maybe it shouldn't, but I'm dealing with reality.

Monday. Today was a light day. My three history classes went to the career center. I used the time to make up the test on Chapter 13, which I will give on Wednesday. Tomorrow they are involved in career stuff again, so no history classes.

Today we had an assembly which presented a combination of anti-drug, anti-alcohol, and trust and accountability lessons with some of the golden rule thrown in. Most of the students said they thought it was stupid, but I noticed during the assembly, the auditorium was very quiet, and the message may have been effective for some.

I had a talk with one student who complimented me on the lecture/discussion format we use. I like hearing that, and am feeling better about that approach. It forces some involvement by the students. It's like doing push-ups: they may not be a lot of fun, but you've got to do them if you want to gain something.

I'm a couple chapters ahead of the other teachers in History, but I'm behind where I'd like to be. We're about one-third of the way through the book but we're over one-half of the way through the year. I intend to skip freely through many chapters so we will get to the 1980s by the end of the year.

I noticed today that the several new kids in my history classes may feel a bit out of the circle because I've been developing a rapport with the other kids since September. I really need to be aware of that and make them feel included. That could go for any new student at any time of the year.

I went to the Junior Prom on Saturday night for about an hour and roamed around taking candid pictures of the kids. My goal is to get two copies of each picture, keep one for a scrapbook and give one to the kid in the picture. It was fun, the kids seemed to enjoy it, and I think it's important to see and be seen by the kids outside the classroom. The pictures, incidently, turned out lousy.

I'm on the verge of actually making out an entire semester plan for the teen law class. This appears to be a mature group, and I want to have a product to match. Now that I'm getting home earlier each day because basketball is over, I'll have time to prepare better.

The Sophomore basketball banquet is Wednesday night. I hope it goes well. By saying that, I guess I'm implying that it might not. I don't know what might go wrong, but I still sense some of the parents may not be happy with the lack of playing time their son got. Gotta quit worrying about that. I did the best I could. I've ordered 15 copies of the team picture I took before our last game and will give one to each player along with a certificate the school has prepared.

Tuesday. A weird sort of "non-day." My three history classes didn't happen because of career counseling. I used the extra hours to get ready for my wife's birthday party and do a little class prep work. Tomorrow I will give a test in those three classes, so on Thursday, it'll seem like a long time since we had a regular class. That's because it has been.

My teen law class is still a good group, and are diligently paying attention to and participating in the lecture/discussions. I don't have a good enough plan for this group. I will have them do something other than take notes tomorrow and will have a test Friday, or Monday.

We had a department meeting after school. The agenda for the meeting was a vote on whether we as a group — there are eight of us — want to keep *Channel One*. The controversy is over the commercials. Some parents in the community are violently opposed (I heard that a shoving match broke out at a public hearing on this topic.) to this forced commercialism in the school. One parent didn't like that one of the ads was for a movie coming "to a theater near you" which showed a barechested man kissing a woman. That parent ought to walk down the 400 hall between classes. But it's good — no, required — that parents involve themselves in what their kids are exposed to.

Other agenda items included whether students ought to be allowed in the faculty lounge. New business was about an assembly committee to help set up, recruit and/or screen school assemblies; bus safety; a review of some proposed new texts; and whether we should change our method of copying, by going to some sort of copy center. It was a very informal meeting involving people who have no hidden agendas.

That may be an example of administration at it's best.

Thursday evening. Last night we had the basketball banquet, and all went well. Actually, it went better than well. Fourteen out of 15 of the kids showed up, (about the same for the Freshman program), and with families, there was a crowd of about 80. Everything and everyone was cordial. I even got a nice card, and there were some fantastic desserts. I look forward to coaching again next year if they'll have me. I guess that closes the book on coaching for this year.

Several simple things are hitting me. I'd like to know more about my students' background, so I can be more effective on an individual basis. That's impossible for all, but for some, it'd be a good idea.

A teacher who deals with students who have learning disabilities told me that he'd like me to tape record my classes, so one student can go over it slowly later. Wow. I don't mind doing that, and I hope the fact that we are being recorded doesn't chill anything. I suppose it's potentially a big question, but if the kid needs it, then it should be done. That's what we're here for.

I started a weekly planning book today. I began filling it in. It'll be a long process, but one I'll be glad I did. However, much of what I do can be summarized by something like, "Thursday, lecture/discussion on Chapter 12. Goal, have students get the basic facts of 'X' and understand how that relates to 'Y'." For example, today in History we started an area of the text called Industrial Growth. This is after Reconstruction following the Civil War. I intend to skip through several chapters very quickly, and the next test will cover topics from the next four chapters. To get us started today, I simply had the kids list things related to industrial growth, such as market needs, labor availability, transportation, materials and technology available, etc., and then had them apply all of that and more to starting a business. It was a fairly good day, but nothing you could make look good in a lesson plan. More planning would help, but running a student-involved socratic discussion is best if not limited too much, and sometimes we go into uncharted waters. But I will try to get more of a written plan ahead of time.

The law class had a "Law in the News" exercise. Kids had to pick out news articles dealing with legal cases and discuss aspects of the case. That type of assignment works much better with this group than with my law class from last fall. These guys actually do it.

My math class took a test today, and all did very poorly. That's a reflection on me, and I intend to change some things about the class. It's a very loose group, and I intend to treat them more like a real class tomorrow. I will walk them through these problems (again) and make sure they get it. Then, they will re-take the test next week. No sense moving on if they didn't get it. And I'm ahead in the book as far as a yearly schedule goes.

Sunday night. We had a health emergency in my wife's family, so we left for the weekend. There I was, sitting in the passenger seat, correcting history tests by the mile. This is a three-day week-end and I was determined to actually get ahead with planning lessons for a couple weeks and do some extra reading in history and education issues. None of that will actually happen.

In Math, the kids were very attentive to the idea of going over the test problem by problem, step by step. A couple thought it was slow and boring, but some thought I was going too fast, and wanted to get it. Well, maybe "wanted" is the wrong word, but at least realized they should get it.

For some reason, kids think that a sunny Friday means a day off. Each period. I was proud of myself for sticking to my guns and moving ahead with the plan in each class. I'm not being paid to waste 20 per cent of the week, and I need to stay on the right side of the line between being their teacher or their buddy.

The more I analyze it, the more I like the method of requiring note taking. It's the push-up, and they have to do it. It's good for various levels of students. Each can get into it as much as they can, and that method is not affected by the varying reading levels. And then jumping sideways into discussions of how our topic is tied in with current events and things going on in the kids' lives makes it better. But it is work, for all of us.

In Law, I made a last-minute change. I figured we weren't ready for the test on Friday, so I moved it to Wednesday. Monday is a holiday, and Tuesday would've worked, but having a test the first day back after a three-day weekend seems inappropriate. I can easily "fill" Tuesday with relevant stuff, and have the test on Wednesday.

✏22nd Week: Feb. 15th - 19th

It took about 22 seconds to be reminded that getting any real performance out of the kids meant giving an assignment they were responsible to turn in.

Tuesday morning. I got home late last night from an unusual meeting. About three weeks ago, I got called to see if I wanted to go to a W.E.A. (Washington Education Association) meeting to be involved in setting goals for the teachers' union. I should point out this is a different group than the local group I referred to earlier. In the local organization I was nominated for an office, but I'm so new at this that I didn't feel qualified, so I declined to get involved.

Regarding this W.E.A. meeting, I was told I was called randomly, and there would only be about ten at the meeting, which will have representatives from about 4 counties. Reading between the lines tells me that they called about 250 veterans who knew how those things went and had the sense to say "No." A combination of curiosity about the direction of the union and a desire to try to help — not to mention the offer of a free dinner — led me to agree to go.

There were about eight teachers and one secretary there, all of us brainstorming about reworking our "Mission Statement" and goals. The group was very cordial. We unanimously decided the union needs to change its focus and image from one of being concerned only about our pay level to a group that is concerned about quality education for kids. It was about a two-and-a-half hour discussion which ended with some nice phraseology about what the W.E.A. should be. But the real question is how or when will anything be implemented?

A scary part of the evening is that I had what I think was a migraine headache at the end. The joke would be that that's what you get for getting involved in union stuff. But it was no joke — I was concerned about my health, and even for a bit about my ability to make the one and-a-half hour drive home. And whether I'd be ready to teach this morning. It cleared up once I went to bed, but it remains a concern.

Yesterday I used the prospect of that meeting as my topic in history. I told the kids that I'd be going to that meeting, so we talked about what unions do, specifically what they accomplish for their members, how life would be different without them, and related issues. The common statement among the students was that the one thing the W.E.A. does is provide too much protection for teachers who have been teaching forever and shouldn't be in the classroom anymore. That was one of the concerns of one of the teachers at the meeting. He said we need to build in a better review or policing of our own before someone else does it for us.

Wednesday. In my mailbox was a form to fill out on whether I intend to come back next year. Next year? I'm wondering about making it through this week. I immediately checked "yes" and got it back to my principal. I hope he's checking a box somewhere that says "yes" to inviting me back.

I got a call midway through the morning asking if I would "substitute" for a teacher on campus during 4th period, which is my free period. I said yes and went to his room at the right time, monitored what was going on and chatted with a few of the kids I knew. It took me back to my substitute days and frankly showed me how far I've come in being comfortable and in control in the classroom.

I discovered one of my students lied to me about going to see a counselor. She actually just skipped out for a half hour. I talked with her about that and pointed out my options, such as writing up a "referral" which would result in some detention, or handling it "in house." I treat my students with respect so long as they treat me with respect. I handled it in house, after conferring informally with the discipline vice-principal to make sure there wasn't a bigger problem going on which her office wanted to be involved in.

Thursday evening. At no particular time today, the thought occurred to me that I like all my classes better this semester. First period is bigger, but also more lively. That class has my biggest, and seemingly only, critic in it. At least she's the only vocal one. I am giving less credence to that student's thoughts than I am to my own beliefs that I'm doing an okay job. Not perfect, but fine.

I resolved (again) last night that I didn't want to do the standard lecture format in history for a couple days. I felt very relaxed in deciding to make a study guide for them to work through instead of listening to me. One of my new students jokingly complained about it because taking notes may actually be less work. One student clearly expressed that he liked getting away from note taking. I'll continue to do both. I should point out that having them work on a study guide is not a "day off" for me. I wander among the class checking progress and talking with students.

The idea keeps recurring that we should make a video of our class, or some kind of video, and have a "pen-pal" class somewhere in the world, and exchange thoughts, etc. via video. I hope it happens.

I need to get this semester's class list on my grade disk, and get some grades posted. Maybe over the weekend.

There was a faculty meeting a couple days ago. The topic came up about our salary structure. I make $3,000 less on our local schedule than I would if our district used the state schedule. The schedules are different because under our schedule, the money is distributed lighter for the first years and heavier after a teacher has more experience. Apparently it's up to each district to decide which they'd like to do. Obviously, I'd like to switch to the state schedule. Given that I'm starting at age 41, I may never get to the later years on the schedule.

I had a discussion with a veteran teacher about that and the fact that apparently some teachers resent that there are teachers who have spouses who also work — often as teachers. Not only do they have double the salary, they're looking at double the retirement benefits. I don't sense any ill feelings on our campus like that. There's no need for any. I see it as a matter of choice. My wife and I agree that her staying home with the kids is of much more value than money. Someone else thinks differently, that's their right, especially when they're paying for our food stamps when we're 67.

I did a newspaper assignment today on President Clinton's tax package. They each were assigned to make a list of ten points about his plan for debate on Monday. Because of the sudden change in plans, this lesson will take up Monday, also. What I really notice is that it's amazing that I'm even worried about it taking an extra day. My memory from the first of the year is that I was looking for ways to fill the days. Is that progress?

At the varsity basketball game last night I saw a student who was not in my class yesterday. It made me mad because I've gone out of the way to help him, and now he pulls this. Today, I found out he had an excused absence for half the day dealing with a family problem. I'm glad I held my tongue, and I'm glad for the type of relationship that develops where I feel close enough to (some of) them to feel personally betrayed or encouraged depending on what they do.

111

✐23rd Week: Feb. 22nd - 26th

Today at a car lot, I met a nice older lady who is looking for a van like ours ... I got her name and called her this evening. So why is this in the teaching journal? It turns out she's a retired long-term teacher ... After we talked cars, we talked teaching, and she had some good advice ...

Monday evening. Today in my history classes, we discussed the points of Clinton's tax proposal. All went well, except in 1st period. Some of the guys in the corner were not as involved as they could've been, and I didn't do enough to bring them in. Afterward I talked to the least attentive one and told him that there are no re-takes of tests this semester and that I won't be carrying people like I did last time. He said okay. I'll wait and see what happens.

In all the classes there was a good discussion about the effect Clinton's proposals will have on various groups. There seems to be a good cross-section of society in the classes, so we got all sides. Now, how do I deal with all this material on a test? That hit me, so I made sure that in all three classes, we discussed at least two comparable issues in depth. There, a fair test question for all classes.

One of my students announces she is going to run for President one day. I encourage her.

A dog wandered into the room at the end of my first period class. No owner, no warning, just a dog. I don't know how the door got opened, and I don't really care. Besides, I'm always looking for unusual guest speakers. Anyway, another teacher noticed it, called the office, and got the instruction as to our options: either take the dog to the humane society or put it outside. I hope it didn't get too cold.

I'm starting the criminal law section of Teen Law. We had a discussion on which actions should be crimes, and if so, how seriously should they be punished. We had all the desired responses, which led into the lesson on intent as an element of crime.

Today at a car lot, I met a nice older lady who is looking for a van like ours. I was there because I am looking for a bigger van and will be trying to sell ours. We overheard each other talking with the salesman. It was a comedy watching him trying to keep us apart, but I got her name and called her this evening. So why is this in the teaching journal? It turns out she's a retired long-term teacher. You know her, the kind who taught you, your dad and barely missed your grandfather. After we talked cars, we talked teaching, and she had some good advice. Even though it's not necessarily new, it's nice to get confirmation from a veteran source. She said that teaching works best when you are yourself, and when you are kind. A nice summary.

Tuesday. I went in this morning at 4:00 to get some things ready. Occasionally that paranoia hits, I can't sleep, so I head in to take care of business. This time I went in to confirm that things were ready, because I had some concern that they weren't. They were, but I used the time to enhance and supplement what I had planned, and it made the day go better.

During lunch, another teacher came in to chat a bit, and wandered around reading my desks. I should point out that a common problem in school is that kids write on desks. Anyway, he read one desk on which a guy had written that so-and-so "sucks," except he misspelled sucks. Maybe he should take remedial vandalism.

During the middle of 3rd period, I got a note that the principal was calling an emergency faculty meeting for today after school. This was a first this year, and of course some faculty were buzzing with possibilities, with everything from a new or resolved sex allegation against a teacher to a *Channel One* vote to an AIDS problem. The announcement was that a student at the school, who is not currently attending, has tested positive for HIV. My immediate reaction was to recall the fight I broke up, remembering that blood was involved, and that the victim has not been in school since then. Wow, that hit home. I was relieved when we were told it was a female, but the gravity of the situation and sorrow for the student were the main concerns. In any event, teachers are all at risk to some degree dealing with as many people as we do everyday, especially, and possibly only, if you are involved with stopping a bloody fight or cleaning up afterwards. At the meeting they handed out rubber gloves and each teacher now has at least a couple in their desk. I grabbed extra ones for my car, too. The risk is real, and it's close.

There will be questions from the kids regarding that meeting. This is a perfect opportunity to show them that actions have consequences.

Following that meeting, there was a coaches' meeting to discuss salary issues. I didn't have any issues I wanted to present, but I wanted to learn, and I did. We're paid on a scale which assumes some sports are worth more. Some coaches were a bit miffed, and another meeting was scheduled. I don't know how many coaches there are at the school. Probably about 30. There were seven at the meeting.

Wednesday evening. There has been no mention or rumblings among the students about the HIV issue. I hope to use it as a time for a positive statement about morality and consequences to actions if it does become a topic of conversation in the halls.

I don't like the test I'm giving tomorrow in history. It covers three chapters, and has no real flow. Maybe I tried to cover too much. I'm going to do another group of three chapters next, so I'll see if there is a trend in having unsatisfactory tests covering multiple chapters.

I had the Teen Law class "brief" a case today. It went well, and for the most part, they wrestled with it just like they're supposed to. That would never have worked with the group I had first semester.

I have noticed that doing a study guide, which is really just questions students answer covering a section of the text, is an easy way to get through the day in history. I do 20 minutes of work once instead of leading a lecture/discussion 50 minutes three times. I haven't done it much, and don't intend to do it much, but it's available as a break in the action, though continuous monitoring is involved. As someone said, "One man's study guide is another man's busywork."

One of my students in History complimented me. She said that this semester she is retaining the information and goes home and talks it over with her parents. She said with a former teacher she wasn't able to do that. That makes me feel good, but it also makes me think about the kids I had last semester who are telling a different teacher about how much better they like them.

Thursday. I've noticed a slight increase in the maturity level of the kids. I mean slight. Then I thought, they are all six months older than they were at the start of the year, which for many of them is one-thirtieth of their lives, and a very significant one-thirtieth at that.

The student council is apparently going to have some funds to up-grade the school's appearance. The idea was proposed to plant some flowers and shrubs around, but that got nixed because it was a given that some kids would ruin them immediately. I thought, it's too bad we give in to the bad guys so easily. Then I thought, the same thing would apply downtown, and it's not just the student population which has its destroyers.

I had a problem today. I was too nice to a student. I allowed her to leave early, to supposedly go to the office, and she was seen driving around. She then claims I said it was okay. Administrators talked to me and indicated that it's a common problem with that student, and to not be too generous with favors. I learned.

I envision a veteran teacher or administrator reading this journal and getting a bit bored saying, "Why am I reading this? I go through this stuff every day." That's the point. To show what goes on everyday.

I gave the test in History today. Many kids were not available to take it, so I will give it to them tomorrow. That ruins a class because I can't lecture when I know 15 percent aren't there. It'll force me to give them all seat work, with some innovation. I could get a policy that make-ups on tests are done during lunch or something. I will think about that.

Friday night. It was donut morning in 1st period. We had taken a collection on Thursday, and I put in enough for about three donuts. They all got taken by other people. Too bad that happens and will cause a need for a sign-up sheet for people who have paid. I get testy over a stolen maple bar.

An administrator was telling me of a problem with a particular student who has a personal dislike for her. My view is that the kids have their own things going on, and we adults in the system need to have pretty thick skins.

I talked with the discipline vice principal about two guys I saw with chewing tobacco, which is against our school rules. She pointed out that one of the guys is on probation, and she didn't know if she wanted this infraction to be the one which may help put him out of school again. I'll wait to hear back from her. I did my part.

Sunday evening. I went out of town for the weekend and talked with a friend who knows I'm in my first year of teaching and wanted to talk about public education. His position is that we all should hold the kids to the standards required in the best private schools. It wouldn't work, but I do feel convinced that I'm not challenging the kids enough.

✏ 24th Week: Mar. 1st - 5th

It's getting old having my lesson plan come to me at 5:00 in the morning. It's not that I don't have something planned, but there's a nagging feeling that with a little more effort, it could be much better.

Monday night. The Junior counselor was in for all of the history classes again, so I didn't teach for three periods today. Some would call it a day off, but I'd rather be into the routine. It gets slow and boring.

For Teen Law I went to the courthouse today and got the U.S. Supreme Court cases for *Plessy v. Ferguson* and *Brown v. Board of Education*. I hope to use them to show how cultures change. I also told the kids I hope to arrange a field trip to the state Supreme Court, an all-day deal. It's okay with my administrators, and I found out that almost all in the class want to go.

The Superintendent for the district walked in to my math class. Everything was fine, but it does make you stop in your tracks to check what you're doing. I was correcting papers while most of the kids were working on their assignment. He could've come in at a much less productive-looking time.

Tuesday. I was at school before 6:00, going over my history lesson for the day. I'm not satisfied with it. I try to bring in facts from various sources to provide some variety and demonstrate to the students that one source is usually insufficient to get a good picture of any topic.

I got a notice that over one-half of the Junior class will be gone for at least part of the day Thursday. That will affect how I plan out my week.

This journal doesn't really give the full picture of the moment you stand up and face the class. Having a prepared lesson, with papers all in order, is fine. However, given the choice between being totally prepared and without much instinct for the thing versus going only on instinct and ability to think on your feet, I'd rather be the quick thinker anytime. But I rely too much on that, and need to prepare more. The best of both worlds is to have such a command for the subject matter that you can branch off to seize a teachable moment, while being able to relate the detour to the current subject matter.

We had a department meeting today. Seven of eight were there. We discussed things like allowing kids in the faculty room or not, checking out new text books, when grades are due for the upcoming grading period, and HIV training. Also, some emphasis was given to the issue of students being tardy to classes and cruising the halls. Part of that problem is mine, because I don't really have a tardy policy. In fact, I wish I didn't have to be concerned with attendance. However, the kids would really take advantage if they knew they weren't accountable.

One kid got a 95 on the recent history test, compared with the 40s he used to get. That's a nice change, but before I get carried away about what a great teacher I am, I need to remember that another student mentioned to me in private how much he dislikes taking notes in History.

I did a bunch of copying out of old law books (from the county law library) and today's newspaper. This is for my law class. I want to get current law articles about crimes we're discussing to put some meat on the bones of the subject. I also got some state Supreme Court advance sheets, which are cases issued by our state Supreme Court, which I will use basically for the same purpose.

Wednesday. Today was pretty lousy. I wasn't prepared. I had average stuff ready for average lectures, and that's about what happened. History turned better when we were talking about inflation and the currency supply. The kids woke up a bit when I tried to buy something from one of them using a piece of newspaper as currency and had them explain why they'd only take the actual dollar bill. Other than that, it was all pretty routine.

Teen Law was worse, and I even ended about 15 minutes early. I was reminded of a *Saturday Night Live* routine where Dana Carvey is doing President Bush at one of the debates, and "Bush" answers a question with a very short answer. The announcer, someone playing reporter Diane Sawyer, reminds him he has 90 more seconds, so he fills it by repeating himself pathetically. I wanted to avoid that. If it's not there, its not there. I spent an extra hour after school preparing for tomorrow, and I feel better. I am enjoying this evening more, also. Last night was no fun knowing I wasn't real prepared.

In History I re-counted the weeks left and the chapters I wanted to cover. I want to get up to the present for the last week or so of class.

One routine criticism of history classes is that you end up getting through maybe two-thirds of the text, ending with World War II. I decided to skip the next chapter altogether, and move toward my goal.

A student asked if I was going to be teaching a certain class next year. I said probably not, and she expressed disappointment. I guess that's a compliment. At the same time, I checked with the counselor about the number of kids signing up for Teen Law. Even though only a small percentage of the kids had registered, a fairly small number of those had signed up for Teen Law. A kid wanted to leave 5th period early, because we were done, and he isn't in school 6th period because he goes to work. I said "No," that he has to stay in the room because you never know when there will be a call for him. Sure enough, 30 seconds later, a messenger showed up with a "pink slip" for him, meaning he had to report to the attendance office. Whew.

I got a call from a judge who offered a set of lawbooks the teen law class could really use. I went to the courthouse to pick them up, and while there, the judge talked about his days as a teacher. He remarked how his second year was much easier than his first.

Another teacher I don't see very often asked me a new question. Do I feel "adjusted?" I don't know. I think I'm as adjusted as I'll ever be. I could be more prepared, that's all.

Thursday evening. Something happened today which I think might drive some teachers crazy. I have "cut off" a certain student from being able to go to the pop machine because she abused the privilege by going other places and not being honest about it. She was mad at me today for not allowing her the privilege, and — since she was pointing out my faults — pointed out that I was giving instructions to one side of the room without facing her side of the room. It was inadvertent, but I think she was partly right. So I turned and gave the same brief instructions to her side, during which she turned her back and sat sideways in her chair facing away from me. My reaction was — well, I didn't really have one. I just went about my job. I suppose that kind of thing might make someone mad, and a rookie should be ready for it, and not take it personally.

I hate the word "busywork" but it got used again. Some like doing seatwork, some don't. I didn't have a lot of choice today because, again, about half of the history classes were gone today to a college orientation, so it didn't make sense to lecture through some material I'd have to cover again. I wanted to make some progress, so I prepared a study guide/question sheet for those who were there. The absent ones can do it on their own time.

Tomorrow I plan to have us make an "investment" in the stock market. One problem is that I don't know much about it, but we'll do it anyway.

I had a parent meeting after class. Her son likes my class, but she just wanted an update about his progress and likelihood of success. It's nice to see some concern.

It was newspaper day, so for law/events class I had the kids critically discuss some articles dealing with criminal activity. One student asked me about the new law that businesses can't employ minors after 10:00 on school nights. She pointed out that the store where she works does that all the time. I found out who the correct person to contact is, and I'll look into that tomorrow.

Friday night. It's getting old having my lesson plan come to me at 5:00 in the morning. It's not that I don't have something planned, but there's a nagging feeling that with a little more effort, it could be much better. I suppose a self-righteous way to look at it would be to say that it's a good thing that I'm open to improvement and it's good to take the extra care and effort to make the last-minute change in order to have some improvement. That would be self-righteous. And also wrong. The truth is, I'm just not prepared enough ahead of time.

I had the history classes "spend" $2,000 in the stock market today. My department head gave me a few pamphlets on how read the stock market pages and how to pick a good investment. I confessed I'm no expert at it, so we worked through it together. We'll check periodically to see how our investments are doing.

There's a grading period coming up next week, and I'm scrambling to see if I want to give my next round of tests before that, then scramble to get them graded, or, put them off until after the grading period. It's only the first third of the semester, and the grades are only advisory, so I guess it doesn't really matter.

The teacher I replaced was back yesterday to pick up some of his old tests and answer keys. He still teaches in town part time, and needs all his stuff. I'm glad I haven't thrown any of it out, though my room still is a bit of a mess with boxes of stuff piled along one wall. My plan is to wait and see what I'll be assigned to teach next year (if I'm asked back) and at that point make the necessary moves to clean up and throw out some older stuff. A good example of one thing I've learned lies in a cabinet full of old *National Geographic* magazines. One teacher mentioned that next year, they may offer a geography class again, and I may teach it. I'll be thankful for the old magazines with pictures of far-off places. It would be useful for hands-on lessons, I think.

I've noticed a modified version of what I think is called the "Swedish Syndrome," the relationship which develops between a kidnapper and his victim, where the victim comes to rely on the kidnapper. I've only made two discipline referrals all year. In each case, I've seen the kids become more friendly toward me after the referral. Huh? Well, its happened two out of two times. There may actually be a deep meaning dealing with kids wanting to have limits put on them so they feel that someone cares. Another surprise for the rookie.

I'm also a rookie wasting too much time at the end of each class period. Though not as often as earlier in the year, I'll end with five or even sometimes more than ten minutes left in the class, and the time gets wasted. This also is a function of planning, and I intend to fill the minutes better. I know I'm not alone in this because when I've had occasion to wander into someone else's class with five or ten minutes to go I see them sometimes all done and waiting for the bell. I'd still rather use the time.

✐25th Week: Mar. 8th - 12th

Today was a great day, and I became a better teacher. I did what you're suppose to do, that is, be prepared with interesting stuff and have aggressive fun with it. I got down to business, the kids could sense that, and we all were more productive. Over the course of a year it may seem that 25 weeks is too long to wait for that kind of progress, but when seen over the course of a career, maybe that's not such a long time.

Monday. I realize that sometimes as I'm preparing a lesson or things I want to get across in a lecture, I'll be thinking of what my most critical two or three students will think about it. That's wrong. It stifles me a bit, and takes the fun out of it. Makes me less effective for the other 28 involved. You can't be worried about pleasing someone who won't be pleased no matter what you come up with.

I showed the first half of *Inside the Jury Room* in Teen Law today. The kids weren't thrilled that I had a handout prepared with questions for them to answer about the movie. They actually had to watch and do something with the information. They paid attention, and it all worked. Incidently, I stopped the movie occasionally to make sure everyone understood so we'd all be staying up with it. I think that's important with any video.

In History I gave a lecture with a couple of handouts for the kids to deal with so they'd know what they were supposed to be doing.

I had I a high-level intellectual victory. One of my students couldn't get her locker opened. I whammed it (sorry janitors) with my knee while pulling on the latch, and it opened. Ta da. Not too many chances to be a hero anymore. Take 'em when you can.

Someone during the day had drawn a pornographic drawing on the chalkboard. The drawing was very vague, but with the right (or wrong) imagination, you could see the intended drawing. Kids in 5th period started giggling, and someone pointed out the drawing. Some girls loudly expressed disgust. I told a guy to erase it, which he did. Lesson: be aware of the stuff going on in your room.

Tuesday night. I decided I will give the next test in History on Monday. I had to figure for Thursday or Monday (Friday being an in-service day). I'll be gone Thursday, so I could have a sub give the test. But I have a movie checked out from the district which I have to turn back at the end of the week. So, I figure I'll have the sub show the movie on Thursday, and I'll give the test Monday. But giving a test Monday after a three-day weekend probably breaks several unwritten rules.

It's election time for next year's Associated Student Body officers. The candidates are spreading brochures around. Here's a sample of what issues concern the kids as derived from one candidate's platform: Goal Number 1: To inform the community about what's going on at the school. The last bond levy failed, and to get more positive public exposure, the candidate is pushing for a monthly column in the local newspaper. 2: To have a place on campus where the Senior class can leave their mark. The traditional painting of the auditorium roof with graffiti has been nixed by tighter night security, and this candidate and the principal are meeting to come up with an agreeable alternative. 3: In-school day care. This needs to be explored because of the increased number of pregnancies at school. 4: Dances and gays. The candidate proposes that the administration and the students need to come up with some agreement as to how to deal with the issue of gay couples, if there are any, being able to attend dances. The rule so far has been that only people with dates of the opposite sex can get in. 5: An Espresso machine. Other schools have them and they are a financial success. And they'd be great on cold mornings when you could use a hot wake-up. 6: Condoms at school. He recognizes that this is a touchy subject, but feels that it's up to the students to let the administration know where they stand. 7: Cafeteria waste. The little cardboard trays and other areas of recycling are ignored. He would rather upgrade to something reusable. In addition, this candidate had an interesting comment: He admitted that he, like everyone else, gets sucked into the social black holes in the school. An interesting description.

A kid in math class suddenly walked out of class, leaving a trail of blood. I didn't see or hear anything because I was in the back of the room helping a student. I discovered it had something to do with someone grabbing a pencil out of someone else's hand, which resulted in a cut. I gave him some bandages and a paper towel, and the bleeding stopped. I intentionally stayed away from the finger and the blood. But a few minutes later, the finger started swelling so I told the student to report to the office. He refused because he didn't want anyone to get in trouble. I told him that wasn't the purpose, that the purpose was to get attention for his possibly broken finger. He said he'd go later. That didn't satisfy me, but since by then there were only a couple minutes left in class I didn't force the issue. Between classes I went to the person in charge of those things and turned in a referral, so I did my job. They would take it from there. I don't know what the result is.

I'm going to be gone Thursday, so I went to the office today to fix up my substitute folder. Being away from school for a day is much harder than being there. That's because you have to have total preparation and organization so the sub has a smooth day. Perhaps that's the prep level I should seek every day. In a sense it is, but many of my days are filled with lecture/discussion with the kids, and much of that, though from an outline, is spontaneous. Wild results aren't necessarily the product of no planning.

Today in Teen Law, I showed the second half of the movie *Inside the Jury Room*. Afterward there were about ten minutes left for discussion. I announced that there was the test Thursday, and that we still had to cover a certain list of topics before the test. I told them I'd lecture on part, but they were responsible for outlining the rest. Only about three or four people worked on that during those ten minutes. I will put a couple test questions in there on those topics to reward the diligent.

I took one student aside earlier in the day to chide him about being prejudiced against one person in our school who is a bit different. I told him straight on that the comments I had to offer were half-personal and half as a teacher educating a student. I told him in no uncertain terms that his comments/actions were sickening and I didn't want them as part of my class or my life. He seemed to listen politely.

This is an unusual entry. It's now Thursday evening. I left town right after a mandatory AIDS seminar right after school on Wednesday. I wasn't prepared for the emotions I experienced today while I was gone, worrying about how things were going for the sub. During the day, I would occasionally check the clock, note what "period" it was in teacher-time, and wonder what was happening in that class. It's good to be concerned, yet worrying doesn't help. I left all the instructions and materials necessary, so I have no reason to believe anything would go wrong.

After I got back in town today, as soon as possible, I went to my room to make sure all was well. It was, but there was one unusual note. It was from a student claiming that a few students had cheated on the test I had left for the sub to give to the class. They had cheated by using the law notebook we were using as a text, rather than by just using their own class notes, which I allowed. I called the teacher across the hall at home tonight to try to find out who the sub was so I can get more facts to deal with it.

Tomorrow is an "in-service" day. I will be at a coaches' clinic all day. That will satisfy my in-service hours, so I get paid for the day. You don't have to be there, but if you don't take the classes offered, you don't get paid.

I need to get the history test ready by tomorrow (Friday) for copying so it'll be ready on Monday morning first period. I hope three things: that I get the test done tonight, though I am very tired from my 24-hour trip out of town and my hurry back for a swimming birthday party for one of my kids; and that the copy room is open tomorrow. If not, I'll hustle in early on Monday morning and hope the machines work so I can get the tests copied by 7:45.

Friday evening. Earlier in the week a student asked if I'd be the faculty advisor for a new political group on campus. I told him a definite maybe, and probably yes. Time, time, time. But I like this particular student's willingness to speak out in class and would like to help.

Today was not school, but the coaches' clinic. I did get the test completed for history, and took it in for copying this morning before the clinic. Two of the three machines were broken down, so I copied the test on the third, slowest machine. I finished copying four pages of the test, times 85 students (over three periods) at about 7:58. That gave me two minutes to lock the tests in my room and hustle up to the gym to the clinic. It worked, but it is an example of how you are on a minute-to-minute schedule sometimes. I'll enjoy the weekend better knowing the copying is done and I won't have to compete with the usual Monday morning crowd.

The clinic speaker was a veteran coach telling us about motivation and other coaching skills.

A side comment. In the beginning of the year it seemed I was primarily worried about filling the time. Now I am more often bothered that there isn't enough time.

✎ 26th Week: Mar. 15th - 19th

Kids dealing with hostile home environments seems so prevalent that all our talk about lesson plans and Bloom's taxonomy sometimes seems silly, like rearranging the deck furniture on the Titanic.

On Sunday night before this week started, an unexpected thing happened. It could've resulted in a problem, but didn't. I was at a restaurant waiting until it was time to go pick up my kids from a nearby church. I heard a basketball game on TV and went into the lounge to watch for a few minutes. I realized I wasn't going to be there long and wasn't going to order any food or drink, so it probably wasn't a great idea to stay in there. As I wandered out of the bar, one of my students came around the corner and saw me. I hadn't thought about that at all because drinking was not on my mind. But it could've looked real bad. I want to be an influence for the kids, and would want them to be discouraged from going into the bar scene. Our actions speak very loudly, and we — teachers or anyone else who would affect youth — must be careful.

I gave the history tests today. Many students indicated they needed more time, and that the tests are getting longer. It's tough to judge an hour-long test, especially when no matter how long or short the test is, some kids will be done in 15 minutes and some wouldn't finish in two days.

After school I worked on getting two guest speakers for the law class. A state legislator also returned my call, and I look forward to getting him in class soon.

I caught myself talking to a few students during the day to find out how last Thursday (the day the sub was here) went. All said it went fine. I got no other indication of kids cheating on the test, and got an explanation of why some students thought some others were cheating. They used their own notes, which were in the front of the notebook they weren't suppose to use. That sounds consistent with the statement that kids didn't use their notebooks, just their notes. And their grades didn't seem different than before, so I'll drop it.

Today a full role of tape made it from my desk to the garbage can in the hall. I saw a kid next to the can, others in the class said he did it, so

I confronted him. He denied it, and I had no choice but to turn him in. I talked with the discipline person about whether that kind of thing is what they want to get involved with, and I was told "Yes." After dealing with the assistant principal, the kid came back to me with an apology and a slightly modified version of what happened, but he admitted he was wrong. That's a good start.

Somewhere during the day I had the thought, "What if these were my kids?" My immediate answer is that I am being too easy on them. And I allow too much crap to go on in the class. For instance, in Math, while the kids are supposedly working together quietly on problems, two girls continually talk as filthy as any X-rated movie regarding graphic sex tales. They chat between themselves, but just loud enough to be heard. I've tried to think of some credible way of telling them that type of behavior isn't appropriate, but I can't come up with any explanation that won't sound like an old fuddy teacher just preaching at them. Today I decided, though, that there are two wrongs here, and righting one of them will be better than doing nothing. I don't live in a cesspool at home, so I shouldn't be forced to live in it at school. More importantly, the students who overhear that stuff shouldn't have to put up with it. I won't change the girls' attitudes, but at least I will clean up the air in my class. And taking a stand is important. We'll see what happens.

Wednesday night. The thought I had a day or so ago about, "What if these were my kids?" kind of woke me up. It made me want to be tougher and get more out of my students. I feel a slight change in my approach, as indicated by my actions today. I did talk to the girl who was the leading "smut talker." I told her I didn't want to run her life, but I am going to run my classroom, and her kind of talk had no place anywhere, let alone in my class, and I won't allow it. She knew I meant business.

We had a guest speaker in Law today. A detective — different than the one I had in earlier. It went fine, and the hour went too fast. I was reminded by another teacher that guest speakers don't always work out. Luckily, a detective is a safe bet to hold the interest of the kids.

Someone stole a box of candy that one student was selling for a fundraiser. It happened between classes, and I got several calls from the vice principal during class trying to find out who it might have been or who might have been in a position to see something. I didn't notice anything.

I have about three hours of papers to correct for History. Instead of doing it all at home at night, I don't feel bad using part of class time to work on them. That's what I intend to do.

As I struggle with the question of whether I am doing a good job, I always think there must be more innovation available. There probably is, and as I get more experience, I'll discover and use it. Meanwhile, I had a good thought today. How many senses do we have? I think it's five: sight, hearing, taste, touch and smell. Those are the only ways we can receive outside stimuli. Only two of those, sight and hearing, are reasonably available in teaching Social Studies. Okay, I guess I could round up a Civil War uniform and pass it around so the kids could smell and touch it, or do some similar physical lesson, but realistically there's not much beyond sight and sound. And the sight method, with the exception of an occasional video or guest speaker, is reading. The hearing method is almost exclusively hearing someone talk. That's usually me, and that's about all who's available. Guest speakers, videos or tapes can sometimes be used. I guess I've gone through this analysis to reassure myself that I'm doing all I can do given the parameters I deal with. Homeschoolers can be released for days at a time to experience something in more natural settings, but that is not possible for my classes, given our current structure.

Today I went for a run while the kids were setting up for the track meet tomorrow. It was fun being among the students outside the classroom. I'll be one of the timers/helpers at the meet tomorrow.

Yesterday I went to the county courthouse to take some law books back to the library. The only other person there was the attorney I'm scheduled to have in as a guest speaker next week. I thanked him ahead of time for agreeing to come in and commented how hard it is to get people from "real life" to come in. He commented that being a teacher is very much "real life." I appreciated hearing that.

Friday. I got in to the room about 6:00 a.m. to correct papers for about an hour and a half.

This morning, one of the seemingly more hostile kids came up to my desk and started talking about problems in his life. He's looking for a different place to live because of the abuse at home. I was glad he opened up a bit and that I had a chance to be encouraging, but I couldn't do much more. That type of problem is so prevalent that all our talk about lesson plans and Bloom's taxonomy sometimes seems silly, like rearranging the deck furniture on the Titanic.

In History, we went over the tests, and I took an extra minute to give the kids a hint on how to do better on the next test. The room became silent. That is something they were interested in. My advice was aimed at their motivation level. I reminded them that, like it or not, they were going to be in the room for about 55 minutes each day. They might as well be diligent during class time, because, if they aren't, they'll have to do the work later anyway. I also had some practical advice on note-taking, and how to review for the tests.

I had a discussion with our discipline vice-principal about her role and the changes that have gone on in school. One of those changes is that schools and police maintain full communication regarding some kids who are involved in crime. It seems we could have a full-time police officer doing what she gets stuck doing much of the time.

One of my students commented on how relaxed I was in comparison with her other teachers, or specifically compared with one teacher. I take that as a high compliment. It doesn't help to be tight, stressed or nervous. Not that I'm not those things often. Maybe I just hide it better sometimes.

There was a track meet after school. I was one of about 20 or more teachers who volunteered to help do stuff. There are a lot of kids on the track team, and seeing my first track meet here reminded me a bit of that night last fall when I first saw the band practicing. There were kids there working hard in a disciplined program, whom I didn't think would want to do that. It was encouraging. It was also another opportunity to be involved with the kids out of the classroom.

✎ 27th Week: Mar. 22nd - 26th

I was discussing with someone about what would happen if you took the average adult, say age 40, off the street or out of their job and had them follow the routine of a public school student. How long would they last? Not a week.

Monday. Today is how Monday earned its name. The 1st period class was as dead as can be, and all I had to offer was a lecture/discussion, without the discussion. The kids actually paid attention, but the whole thing was dead. The rest of the day got better, after everyone got the Monday morning blues out of them, but it was still a Monday. Tomorrow will be something different.

Even though it felt like a ploddy Monday, something happened that made me realize that even ploddy Mondays have their place. My nine year old had a swim lesson after school at the town pool. He had a substitute teacher — a no-nonsense older women. I could tell during the lesson that he didn't like what was going on, but he stuck with it for the half-hour. The lady obviously has a lot of experience swimming, but my son didn't like the fact that she made him work.

I'd compare that to the classroom. In the process of making the kids do the work, you will cause them to not always like what is going on. But stick with it and make them work.

I was at the library until 4:30 copying a couple cases I got at the law library downtown after school. There is a certain amount of hustling around town to get optional lesson-plan material.

Tuesday night. In math class I got a bit fed up with the crude language of the student I mentioned earlier. When I was questioned about being a bit old-fashioned, I repeated that I didn't live in a cesspool and I shouldn't have to work in one. Some didn't know what a cesspool was, so that had to be explained. Then one kid said that he'd never heard anyone say anything like that. It was about time he did. When one of them needed further explanation about what I meant, a quieter student piped up from across the room with, "He doesn't want to listen to your crap." That pretty well sums it up. It also points out a couple basic schoolroom truths: Kids are listening, even when you think they aren't, and it's okay to take a disciplined line with the kids, because most of the other kids appreciate the result.

A student in my history class asked a great, out-of-the-blue question. Given that about half of all marriages break up, when I got married was I afraid that I'd get divorced? I explained how my wife and I view marriage — as a life-long commitment; divorce isn't an option. That lit a spark in me, and I proposed to the class that we skip a routine chapter later on and use that time for a study of "family." There was overwhelming support among the students for that, but time and extra effort to create a viable "unit" on that will be an obstacle.

Wednesday. There was a news story about a school in Michigan that was closing today, March 24, because it has run out of funding. That's about ten weeks short of the full year. The kids in the program were commenting on how it wasn't a full year and how they wish they could have school. Are my students going to be better off because we *will* have school for ten more weeks? What can I do to make it worth their time?

I talked to a veteran about the line-up next year in our department. No one knows at this point, but I told him I'd like to teach Contemporary Issues and the law classes. We'll see.

I subbed for another teacher during my planning period today. They were watching a movie, and the only reason I mention it is that one kid was being disruptive, so I didn't hesitate to move him. Would I have done that earlier in the year?

My classes later in the day are better. Is that because I am? I don't know, though I do know that I'm going to experiment in History next week. We are going to study World War I in one week, including the test. I've reserved the library for two days, so they can do some independent research, and report to the class. No lectures this time, at least not by me.

I finally finished the book, *Family Matters, Why Homeschooling Makes Sense*, by David Guterson. It had a lot of ideas on how schools could be better. I am interested in alternatives in education for all the standard lofty reasons, and also more selfishly so I can have better classroom experiences myself. Knowing more will help. I think it will give me the confidence to try new things, because failed new things are better than routine, boring old things.

Thursday night. Today I gave a test in my three history classes. As always, it was open notes. I am very tempted to see how the kids would do if I gave the same test tomorrow with no notes and no knowledge that the test is coming. I have other stuff planned, but I still might.

In Law, I had a guest speaker in. There was an article in the local paper about a criminal trial that had just ended, and the deputy prosecutor on that case is the one I had in the room as a guest. Pretty timely, if I say so myself.

What I learned from the hour was that even though having the guest in was a great break from the routine, and the guest happened to be a pretty good, loose speaker, the kids were still only luke-warm. Many appeared down-right bored. They are totally institutionalized.

I'm going through the change from just observing what's going on to having opinions about how public school could be better. The freeing thought is that our system needs much improvement, so it's okay to try anything. I mean anything. If it fails miserably, big deal. The content isn't bad — it's just that by necessity, the delivery is limited, which sometimes causes the reception to be lousy. I was discussing with someone about what would happen if you took the average adult, say age 40, off the street or out of their job and had them follow the routine of a public school student. How long would they last? Not a week. Getting herded from cell to cell each hour on the hour is not the way it ought to be. Soap box done for the moment.

My opinions are not new or unique. The administration at my school shares my concerns — to some degree. There are weekly meetings involving faculty and administration which deal with how to completely restructure school.

Friday night. This morning I was at school at about 6:00, got on the word processor and put my vague idea for my World War I plan into a specific form. Three days in the library on reports, and an open-book, take-home test. I announced this great plan, which incidently is for the week before spring vacation, to very minimal fanfare.

My wife and kids came into the library at the end of one of the history classes. In that class, I'm always talking about my family, and I wanted them to come in one time. The class saw that I have a life outside of school .

I almost lost my temper with one kid today. Instead, I just quietly turned away, sat at my desk calmly, and worked on something. I can't let one bad attitude or moment wreck a class or a career.

I should keep a list of the odd questions I get asked. Today's was, "Does a pig have eyelashes?"

✏ 28th Week: Mar. 29th – Apr. 2nd

My wife and I went to a coffee house guitar performance. I couldn't help but notice the similarities to a classroom. First, the guitarist had to get everyone's attention, then do his thing and hope people caught on. His audience was there voluntarily and were adults, two major differences between what he faced compared with what a teacher faces. But the comparison to being "on" every moment was there. All eyes were on him, as they are on the teacher. Better have your guitar tuned.

Sunday night my wife returned home, from a weekend retreat, freeing me up to do some school work. I made the promised take-home test for my history classes. I got to school early Monday in order to be able to copy the tests prior to first period. Two good things happened: I beat the crowd, and the copy machine worked.

We were in the library 1st, 3rd and 6th periods in History so the kids could work on their brief reports. Most got into the work, though some took some nudging.

On her own, one girl came over to me and mentioned a "purity ring" her father had given her. Wearing that was her promise that she would abstain from sex until marriage. I've heard of those rings, but that was a first as far as discussing it with one of the students. She explained that while they were discussing it her mom cried, and it was a very close moment for their family. She's fortunate to have them.

In 2nd period, a student got up and left to go out to the hall to discuss a problem between her and another girl. The discussion got louder, then physical. I ran out and separated them. In hindsight, I suppose jumping between girls in a fight could open me up to charges of some sort of inappropriate contact with them, but they had to be stopped. It all ended quietly, with referrals to the discipline office.

One of my students is no longer eligible for road trips in baseball because he flunked two of my tests in Teen Law. He wanted to know what he could do. He knew all along. It's just that now he might.

Monday night. I'm not feeling well. If I'm going to get sick, tomorrow is a good day to miss. Library in my three history classes, film in my law class, and math, sort of, in my math class.

I forgot my math book today. The one with the answers. I told the class that, and, knowing my math ability, they hoped and even assumed we'd have a "nothing" day. Nope. The show must go on, and it did. I made the assignment, and we worked through a few problems. We'll correct the papers tomorrow.

Tuesday night. One of the veterans said it feels like spring vacation is about two weeks too late this year. We talked about what to expect after the break, my opinion being that it will be antsy and wild. Another teacher said it depends on how you play it up. If a teacher acts like he has spring fever, the kids will follow suit.

Over the weekend, after receiving stern warnings all year against it, some Seniors painted the roof of the auditorium. It's been the custom, I'm told. Four Seniors are on long-term suspension, and a few others are on five-day, in-school suspension. Some parents were not pleased with the harshness of the penalty, but as one veteran put it, this is a "teachable moment," so next year's Seniors get the message.

There was a department meeting after school. One topic was whether to order a few textbooks for next year, knowing that we are about to do a major order for the following year. I volunteered that instead of giving out 90 texts in my three classes, I'd be perfectly willing — in fact I was going to do this anyway even before I heard there was a text shortage — to keep about 30 texts in my room for the students to use. That way the books would be in the room during class time when there is an in-class assignment.

Other topics included how many TAs (teacher assistants) each teacher should have. I pointed out that I don't use my two TAs well, and certainly don't want more than one. Some agreed with that, some didn't.

Pep assemblies. We all agreed that they should be expanded to recognize such academic activities as Knowledge Bowl and debate. The real question was why even have them, but that topic was nixed when we realized no one asked us to vote on Americana.

I need to get better control of my math class. It's a bit of a disaster regarding content and discipline. I'm too loose, and we're coming up on springtime, which won't make it any better. Easy, just set down some rules and follow them.

Wednesday. There was a faculty meeting after school to deal with, among other things, ending rumors about why those who painted the roof got certain punishment. The teachers were wondering why they were treated so lightly, while the principal explained how he's dealing with parents who think their sons' treatment was too harsh.

Another part of the meeting dealt with a report on whether the school day or year should be restructured, such as going to an all-year school calendar or to more flexible hours so the same facility could serve the growing student population. My reading is that there is generally high enthusiasm among the staff for trying a new ideas in teaching. Some, of course, are not enthused about any change.

I was explaining to a veteran how I was making a rookie mistake this week by having my three history classes turn in a take-home test and two reports by this Friday, the last day before spring break. Guess what I'll be doing part of the break? The veteran agreed it was a rookie mistake — it's okay to give the assignment, but the mistake is to think you need to use vacation time to correct it.

I find myself having a little less tolerance for the disruptive noise and chatting in class, and occasionally use a little more volume, a little quicker than I used to, to bring them around. The kids can sense that, and are responding by tuning in faster when I start talking.

Thursday evening. I haven't kept daily notes for a couple days. Is it getting routine? If so, that's just as valid to report to anyone interested in the day-to-day life of a teacher as anything else.

Today in 6th period, the orchestra, which is going to Carnegie Hall for spring vacation, put on a performance in the auditorium. Attendance was optional, and I took my class. Good show.

I received news that an influential man in my life just suffered a heart attack and is in very serious condition. One thing to learn from that is to go ahead and do stuff while you can. I'm glad I made a career switch and am actually trying education, rather than merely wondering what would've happened if I had tried it.

In Math today, I made a literally last-second switch in the plan. Up at the podium, I realized the lesson for the day was too advanced, so I skipped to one which I had briefly reviewed and found more basic, and assigned that one. I had reviewed the first one and was ready, but something said it wasn't going to work. I went with my gut, and the hour went fine.

In my history classes, I have been urging the kids to get their take-home tests in by today. I told them the very real reason for my request — so I could get them corrected tonight and not have them hanging over my head over vacation. Many of the kids have done that, and my workload over vacation will be lighter. Good. I do want to get all my grades on computer updated and everything ready to go for when we get back from vacation. For History, that means figuring out which chapters or time periods to deal with or skip. The experiment in the library was a success, and I want to build that in some more.

In Law, I started a new section today with lecture and discussion. It was lively and interesting because of the subject matter: assault and battery in the context of civil lawsuits. Most of the kids got into the lesson, but there were some chatterers. I find myself more often talking directly to a chatterer and pointing out to them that it's rude to talk while someone else is talking. Direct, correct, and it works.

For Law over vacation, I'll probably just check the papers for articles dealing with topics we'll be covering in the next few weeks. I suppose I could work a library assignment in for them, but I have got to figure out a specific game plan. As the librarian pointed out regarding times when classes are using the library, it makes everyone's job easier when the kids are given a definite assignment, simply stated. Then we all know what we're supposed to be doing.

Friday night. Today was the last day of school before spring vacation. The day went fairly normally, although I do remember that with about five minutes to go in 6th period, I was waiving my white handkerchief out the window to the equally harried teacher across the walkway.

A student came by my room because he had a few extra minutes and wanted to chat. I liked that. That is an example of something that happens occasionally that I have not included enough of in the journal.

My goal in Teen Law was to present a current-events issue out of the paper, but nothing suitable was in there, so I just forged ahead in our Torts section. The kids hung in there real well.

I "subbed" during my planning period for an absent teacher. There are a lot of people gone today, some because of vacation, most not. I noticed in this teacher's room things were laid out so the kids knew what was expected of them. Also, he had a great movie regarding prejudice. You could hear a pin drop, the kids were so into it.

One of my history students who had been a below-average student until the last test (when he scored a 92) turned in a perfect, typed assignment today. Success does breed success.

I think I'm looking forward to this vacation more than to the Christmas vacation. Probably not so much because of getting away from the routine, but because we have some fun stuff lined up. I'll also spend some time planning for the next two months of school.

✏ Spring Vacation Apr. 12th - 16th

There is still about one-quarter of the year left. I will point that out to the kids, and we'll get to work.

Sunday night following spring vacation. I'm tired. We visited some relatives, then some friends came to stay with us a few days. I went golfing a couple times, which strikes me now as a huge amount of time away from home, but it was fun.

I did manage to correct all past papers and get the grades on computer and printed out for posting tomorrow.

I went to the county library and did some research, as much as you can do with a two year old waddling about emptying bookshelves. I was getting cases regarding some upcoming topics in my law class. I also spent a couple hours reading and planning for History.

I learned a lesson when I left campus this Thursday after going to the track for a run. I wasn't exactly enjoying the vacation because, I realized, I still had some work hanging over my head. I went home and just did it, and the weight was lifted.

I need to realize that we're not yet on the home stretch. There is still about one-quarter of the year left. I will point that out to the kids, and we'll get to work.

✎ 29th Week: Apr. 12th - 16th

They don't know this yet, but I'll give different tests to every other person. There are wandering eyes, and this will solve that. I'll tell them about it before the test, maybe. It's tempting to not tell them and see what happens.

Monday. It's the first day after spring vacation, and no one was really ready. I handed out the papers I did over "vacation." After that, it was show-and-tell time about the kids' adventures during their break. On the high road, the school orchestra went to Carnegie Hall, so they had New York stories to tell. On the other end of the scale one student reported about a party which lasted the entire vacation. Those were the extremes, and there was a bit of everything in between. One guy's brother shook hands with the President, and one girl's dad caught a foul ball at a Cleveland Indians game. You can't beat fun.

In History, one student walked out of class. This is the one who is a bit independent and has been the complainer. Class was just too boring for her. She belongs in the A.P. classes. I went to her advisor to talk about it, and we worked out a plan for some innovation and variety at the challenging level she's looking for. I was naturally concerned about my own teaching ability because I had "lost" a student. Her advisor assured me I was doing fine and, to soothe my bruised ego, gave me other examples of the student's independent behavior.

I'm starting to lose my voice. That's a major issue for a teacher because it can drastically affect planning, let alone the obvious problem of basic communication.

I know I will be gone two days next week for medical reasons, so I made sure to order some videos for the sub to show. They will be in next Monday. That's the furthest ahead I've had to plan.

Tuesday. Sure enough, I had no voice in the morning. To be able to get something done in my classes, I went through the remaining sections of our history chapter and wrote questions for the kids to answer on paper. Another "study guide." I am surprised at how they work their way through them quietly. I did about the same in my law class, having them brief a case. Actually, I'm doing just about as much talking as if it were a normal lecture/discussion because I wander around the room chatting with and hopefully helping the students.

I talked with the state Supreme Court bailiff today and got the word that it would be no problem for the class to be in court to hear oral argument. I will contact him in about two weeks when it is known what cases will be heard on which dates, so I can choose the juiciest day to go. I told the kids about their choices. The court has two sessions: one at 9:00 a.m. and one at 1:30 p.m. Each session includes two cases, which means each session is about two hours or more. We live three hours from the capital, so even if we were going only for the p.m. session, we'd leave about 9:00, which means missing almost the whole day of school, a plum for any student. But surprise! The class overwhelmingly voted to leave school before 6:00 a.m. and be there for both sessions. I was impressed. I will try to get the legal briefs from the attorneys ahead of time so we can be prepared to intelligently follow the arguments. And I'll use these cases as a test source, I think. It could be a good unit, but will testing on it ruin it? Make it too much like school, and take the real life out of it?

I'm thinking more about the student who walked out. In talking yesterday with the counselor, I pointed out that other bright kids don't do that, they simply join in and, in fact, lead the discussions in class. I feel the student who walked out would feel and act the same no matter which of my history classes she was in, even the more talkative ones later in the day. Also, if I need some personal reassurance, I remember that other kids have transferred from other classes to mine. I'm not saying that to brag, but to point out that things like this go both ways.

The arrangement we have invented is that the student will do just about the same work as the other students, regarding handouts and such, and take the same tests. She will be doing some independent projects in lieu of sitting in class.

I used some time during class to wander around — educators would call that monitoring — and chat with students who had work that wasn't handed in yet and needed some prodding.

Wednesday. Today I decided I'd divide the history chapters into sections and have the kids get into groups and teach their section or special assignment. This was a good lesson for me in making sure that all were included, and some were joined with others in a group that they normally wouldn't hang out with. Good. They'll work on their assignments and start presentations Friday.

During my planning period, I decided to call a high school in the Bronx to talk with someone about my idea to exchange videos showing life around our respective campuses. I picked the Bronx because that probably would be about as different as you could get from our Northwest, small-town culture. Our office has a book of all high schools in the country. Once I located New York City, I picked a school at random. I called and talked to a woman in the Social Studies department who was very excited about the idea. I'll send a letter clarifying my thoughts on the project, and away we go. Her principal needs to approve everything, she said. That made me think that perhaps my principal would like to be filled in. I did so, and he likes the idea, too.

I sat in briefly on a school restructuring meeting. I've only attended a couple meetings, so I felt a little like I was crashing the party. The argument today was whether to ask the school district for money to hire a consultant on these things and for an additional in-service day for the teachers to all work on this idea.

Thursday night. A counselor asked me to review the grades of one student, so I checked on my gradesheets and gave him the information. For some reason that caused me to check if my three history classes as a whole were doing about the same. For instance, I checked the recent take-home test I gave, which had 60 possible points. Of those that turned it in, all got somewhere between 50 and 60, and most in the high 50s. However, since some didn't turn it in, the class average was 38.9. 3rd period was 38.2 and 6th period was 39. That amazing consistency made me check the class averages for all work done this semester, and I found first period was 73%, 3rd period was 67% and 6th period was also 67%. Those scores are consistent, but misleading. There are a couple students in each class whose scores are very low, and throw the average down. I have and will continue to be "on" those students to get their work in.

I brought donuts in 1st period. One, I was hungry, so I went to the store and figured while I was there, I'd get some extras. Two, I don't mind doing something nice for the class, though I did have a donation jar for future treats.

Friday night. You can't be too careful when you give directions. A group of my better students in one class did their independent report on the wrong chapter. Since they were Section One in the chapter, we simply halted giving reports, and I gave them and others who needed it a day to work on their topics. In the other two history classes, the reports went fine. Students were in front of the class, using the overhead, and teaching their assigned parts of the chapter. I think it's a valuable perspective for kids to experience. It's just as valuable for the teacher to sit in the class occasionally to get that perspective.

We've had a good discussion in Law the last few days. The Socratic method came out (getting the kids to argue a point, and refining it by asking them questions to clarify and explore other possibilities). I will attempt to do that more often.

There was a home track meet today, and I got to work with a veteran coach helping in the pole vault pit. He had common sense stories to tell about surviving as a teacher, and I learned a lot. Most of it was similar to what the veteran teacher from the car lot said. Be yourself, and be kind. And don't get frustrated when you have the right to.

Today a student who has attendance problems in all classes went to the bathroom and simply didn't come back. I had no choice but to write a referral.

In Math the kids did terribly on a test. I told them that things were going to change, and here's what it's going to be: I will not give them questions which are beyond the scope of the class title, which is Math for Daily Living. Questions will be relevant. I will no longer grade the daily work, nor will they get credit for it. Example: As it is, during class I go over problems, and basically give out the answers. And they all dutifully write down the answers — I'd do the same in their shoes — without really understanding. Even though they get 10s on the daily work, their tests come in at under 50 percent. So now they will be accountable on test day. They don't know this yet, but I'll give different tests to every other person. There are wandering eyes, and this will solve that. I'll tell them about it before the test, maybe. It's tempting to not tell them and see what happens. I can see it now.

"I got the exact same answer as Fred but you marked mine wrong!"

"Right, Bill, but you didn't have the exact same question."

"Oh, uh, huh?"

I'll have to wait and see how devious I feel on test day.

✎ 30th Week: Apr. 19th - 23rd

I read a good thing about honesty today. You can con a con, you can fool a fool, but you can't kid a kid. They see through it.

Monday. I can't believe I just wrote "30th Week." Time is flying, and the first year is almost over. I'll save the philosophizing for later. For now, just the facts.

I'm only going to be in school three days this week. I've got some elective surgery which will cause me to be out of school Thursday and Friday. Last Monday I ordered nine, count 'em folks, nine videos, hoping that at least a couple would be available for my law class and my history classes on the days I'll be gone. I went 0 for 9. I also learned that it was my fault for not getting the order in earlier. Fortunately, the video store which loans out freebies to teachers has one of the law movies I ordered, *12 Angry Men*. I'll be hustling for the history classes.

I just found out that over half of the history classes will be gone Wednesday on something called "job shadow." They tag along with someone in the workplace for a day. That sounds like a good idea. But what do I do with the 40 percent of the three classes who stay behind? I can't lecture or do anything of real substance in class which I will have to re-do for 60 percent of the kids later. My quick solution was to sign up at the library to have my three classes go there, and have everyone write a brief report on how the job they choose to either shadow or look up is affected or controlled by the government. Those going on a shadow can discuss that with their host, and those who stay behind can get the information from the library. Not bad for a quick fix.

I had a discussion with a student who thought I was unfair for writing her up. She was gone for the last 40 minutes of class after I allowed her to use the restroom. I pointed out her history of not returning on time. She eventually agreed I was fair. She was obviously testing me. I guess I've grown enough as a teacher not to need her approval.

A kid paid me back two dollars that I lent him a couple weeks ago. He tried to pay me interest. I didn't let him, but for some reason the thought went through my head about the trouble I'd be in if I did accept the interest, and how it would all come down administratively.

Math was better today, for the sole reason that I did some teaching.

I'm giving a test tomorrow which will be easier than before, and I've decided I'll be giving two different tests, so no student will be taking the same test as the person sitting next to him. Many of the kids don't have calculators, and I can't force them to go buy one, I guess. With two tests, they can share calculators, and still be doing their own work.

Spring is in the air, and the kids are getting a bit giddy. We still have about eight weeks to go, so it'll be interesting.

Tuesday night. We had a department meeting today, and the agenda was how we were going to preview textbooks next year. My choice was to not be one of the two who try a new text on one class and see how they react. My reason is selfish, I think. One, we may not use it again, and it would be a lot of work to outline a new text that you may not use again. Also, I will have one new class, it appears, to prepare for. The preliminary tally is that I'll be teaching three U.S. History classes, one Teen Law and one Contemporary Issues. Just like this year, except trade out Math and put in Contemporary Issues. More work, but I'll look forward to it. The book issue wasn't resolved, but it appears we will be "piloting," that is, trying out, several texts during the year so next spring we can order several sets of new texts.

I gave the math test today. This is the one where I went over each question yesterday, and simply changed a few numbers. The ones who prepared the least complained the most. I have bent over backwards to go slow and help with the methods involved, but some choose not to listen. It will get better.

I had a discussion with a veteran today about our school's hiring process, and the fact that there won't be any new positions next year in our department. We talked briefly about the process involved last year, when I got hired. I told him I realize that this is a plum of a job and was thankful to have it.

I am leaving a movie for my sub to show all my classes while I am gone. I have two pages of questions for them to answer as they watch. That took till about midnight last night.

The kids are continuing to give their reports in history class. One group created a video, and it was a lot of fun. Another group has prepared a *Jeopardy* game. Most did less work, but at least are getting the experience of being up front.

Wednesday. Today was job shadow day, so we were in the library so my history classes could look up how government affects different

142

jobs. One of my better students paid me a compliment, saying that this was a good assignment. Now he perhaps is my best student.

I spent much of the time later in the day getting ready for the sub. No matter how much you prepare, it's always iffy because as we all know, having a sub makes for odd behavior among students. A 16 year old is a 16 year old, and a sub is a sub, and never the twain shall meet.

I talked with a veteran about creating a video library with all of the Social Studies department teachers pooling their resources. He said that has never has happened, that teachers all just kept their own stuff. He was receptive, though. The reason it came up was so that if my plan "A" for the sub didn't work, the sub would then have easy access to a video, and the day could be solved with something on the subject matter we are in. Also, we were both remembering the incident a while back where a sub for a different teacher was frantically running around looking for some relevant material.

Thick skin. You gotta have thick skin. Out of 1,400 kids in the school 1,398 might be great, but the other two ... No matter who you're dealing with, you have to know that pleasing you isn't necessarily high on the kids' list of priorities. As one student put it, "No matter what you come up with for a plan or a solution, someone's always gonna bitch." Some will be trying to drive you to anger, others will simply go ahead with their agenda knowing you're not a "real person" so why worry about your reactions? And they're partially right. You can't focus on yourself, as though all the kids are supposed to somehow think you're the best thing since the three-ring notebook. It won't happen.

Today was a bit busy for a while. During my planning period, I went to the courthouse law library and looked up some cases in the subject we are covering in Teen Law. I came back to school, made 35 copies of the case, and used it in my 5th period class. I needed that because I realized, belatedly, that many of the kids would be gone from school today, so lecturing to half a class wouldn't make sense. Having them brief a case does, because those who are gone can make up the assignment on their own time.

I keep trying, with changes made along the way to try to find something that works.

Monday. Today was a significant day, my first day back after a two-day absence. It's a good thing to have a sub once in a while so you can get an objective look at what is going on in your class. The sub I had is a veteran, well-respected, and I take her notes and comments very seriously and am glad she expressed her concerns.

Her first comment was that the film I supplied was excellent, and it grabbed the kids' attention. Enough of the feel-good stuff.

I later learned that the TV and video stand I reserved and placed in my room had been removed by someone for use in a different class-room. I should have put a note on it, I guess. It appeared as though I hadn't done my job in that respect, though I did take all the proper steps. Sometimes you need to do more. I feel bad knowing that she had to go through a last-minute scramble to get the right equipment.

She also pointed out that it appeared to her that there was a lot of movement in and out of the classroom. Too many people coming and going, like to the bathroom or on a pop run. She discussed that with my bosses, and they in turn talked to me about it.

I learned today that there is a growing, building-wide problem with that. I talked with one veteran about this issue, and he pointed out that it took him about six years to get the right balance of strictness and looseness, and as soon as you get that down, you'll get a class that is of such a different make-up that the rules you've come up with don't seem to fit. His suggestion to me was that things are fine this year, that it wouldn't make much sense this late in the game to try to change the rules. His indicating I wait until next year reassures me that things are not in need of emergency repair, that I'm doing okay. However, I think I'll get a bit more consistent and tough. And next year things will have to be tighter. I am contemplating posting some new rules, though. I don't like that I let it get to the point where someone else has to see it first and relay that information to me through my superiors.

The big news is that on Friday while I was gone, a kid from one of the morning classes went to the restroom and let off or sprayed some sort of pepper mace container. They had to evacuate part of the building for about 20 minutes. The culprit has been evacuated for the rest of the semester. Gone two days and I miss all the fun.

In History, two of the three classes finished up their reports, which didn't go so well today, though I'm still glad kids got the chance to be up front. On the bright side, one student brought a tape of a 1930's radio broadcast to show the culture of the times. It was more fun than people expected.

In Math, the policy of not grading the daily work and just getting ready for the tests is getting a mixed, but mostly negative, review. However, the kids have done at least as much under this system as they did under the old method. The only difference is this time, they do it to understand, not just to copy the right answer once I dish it out while explaining a problem.

Tuesday. Well, today was a learning day. I handed out and posted my Supplemental Class Rules. It listed specific penalties for tardies and indicated I'd rearrange the seating chart if necessary to deal with class noise. Very understated, but I now have a better chance of tightening up on discipline instead of getting slack as we come to spring.

It's too bad it's the 31st week and not the 1st week. I had some ideas of my own back then, I thought they were just right, and I might not have heeded the advice I got today. But I will now. I was talking with a veteran (different than any other veterans I've referred to so far) who told me some of his secrets of dealing with tardies. His solution seems to be a good combination of discipline and subject matter. When the kids come to his class, every class, there is a question on the board dealing with something they did the day before. They have about one minute to write an answer and get it turned in. It's worth x amount of points. If you are tardy, you don't get those points. Also, those questions are always on the test. It pays to show up in his class on time. And the kids are immediately into the flow of the class.

I gave the open-book test in history class today. One of the better students commented that she learned more doing it this way. We did those class presentations leading to this, so I guess it could work.

The math class is trying to get the idea. I think the next test will reveal to them that they need to learn the material as we go in class. I've said it, and demonstrated it, but still several of them are busy complaining about things rather than learning things. I keep trying, with changes made along the way to try to find something that works.

145

I talked with the state Supreme Court bailiff today about the field trip coming up. I also discovered we are short on funds for field trips. I learned that if you want to take a field trip in the spring, do it before spring break. The school district money is used up by then. However, the Social Studies department has some funds available, so we are going to go. The bailiff is going to send briefs of the cases we are going to hear, and we will argue them in class in the weeks ahead of time. I hope it turns out as interesting as it sounds.

During lunch I was in my room with another teacher talking about stuff when a third teacher popped in and told us to stand by, that we might be needed for "enforcement." Unfortunately we knew exactly what he was talking about. Fortunately, nothing happened.

Two exterior door windows got kicked in today. I don't know by whom or when, but those suckers are thick and wired, so someone really wanted them broken.

Wednesday. I had a discussion with my math class about how it should be run. They complained that they were going to be graded on quizzes and tests only, and not on daily work where I give the answers out. They miss the automatic "10" everyday. Well, if I had any doubt about the need for the change, their comments erased them. They need to be in an accountability situation. Even — no, especially — against their will.

A student approached me about the legality of forming an "underground" newspaper. He wanted to do something the school administration might not like, and wanted advice on how to do it, or what they could do. I have no problems against kids expressing their opinion, but I am very supportive of this administration. It put me in a sticky mental moment, and I didn't offer much, if any, advice. Perhaps I should mention that conversation to the administration, but I'm sure every year they face that issue.

There was a faculty meeting after school. The issue again was the appropriateness of the discipline given to students who painted the roof. About 96 percent of the faculty felt the sanctions were too light. We have to live with the consequences of leniency. There is a school board meeting tonight dealing with the appeal by some of the students who are claiming their punishment was too harsh. A few faculty members mentioned they may go to the meeting to express their views.

In Law, we started the contracts section, with a decent interest level in class. We also discussed other matters, such as going to the Supreme

Court and doing the "Bronx Video," which will be a video of scenes from around school.

I had to hustle to the courthouse after school to get lawbooks for cases for the contracts section.

Thursday. I heard that at the school board meeting last night they found some technicality allowing them to reduce the punishment of the kids. I talked with someone on campus about the fact that teachers feel the need to review the discipline guides, and have some input. Something will happen on that soon, I'd bet.

In Math, I gave a quiz today. Not that it matters — I'm certain I have the full confidence of the administration — but after I gave out the quiz, and just as the students were ACTUALLY IN THEIR SEATS WORKING ON THE QUIZ, GIVING THE APPEARANCE OF A STUDIOUS CLASS, in walked the principal. Nice timing. I admitted to him later that was the most organized two minutes the class has ever seen.

There is still a lot of chatter in that class. I talked with an administrator about sending a few of the perpetrators to the discipline office. I explained that I felt it was a defeat for me to have to do that, but it has come to that. I was aggressively assured not to think that way, because the kids in that class have problems in other classes, are getting referrals from other teachers, so I'm not alone. I will do so tomorrow, if they can't follow basic instructions and act civilly. One transient student wrote on his desk — I saw it later — that "Mr. Gish is incompetent." That, I believe, was in reaction to my not keeping the class quiet. I am alleviating that starting tomorrow.

I went to a law office after school to get some books. Every time I'm in that environment, the question about whether or not I'd want to go back to that profession pops up in the back of my mind. The answer continues to be "No," and makes me think of why I got out of it and into teaching in the first place. Unfortunately, the one class that is tough is dominating my thoughts. Allowing that class to be less controlled causes an adversary-like feeling. When I was in Junior High, a teacher mentioned to our rowdy class one day that he had a much better-paying job waiting for him downtown. He said he didn't want to do that, because he wanted to teach, but that if every class was like ours, he'd make the switch. Now I know how he felt.

I graded the math quizzes, and the results are much better than they have been in the recent past. Good, that's part of it. The "deportment" part is next. However, I have had it pointed out to me that other teachers have several periods of worse classes.

In Law, a couple guys came up and asked me about this "deal" they had made. They excitedly went over who said what and wanted to know if that amounted to a valid contract or not. That was a fun, teachable moment, which got shared with the whole class, which became the judge of the case.

I realize two very big things tonight which will help in the classroom-control department. The first is that there will be less chatting among the kids if they are separated by space. That makes sense. The horseshoe arrangement is modern, intimate, and appears to give the room more of a seminar than a classroom appearance. However, it also results in the kids being literally in a desk-touching-desk situation. I really do not like the look of a classroom in rows, but I can now see that it solves a few problems. Also, on test days, it's next to impossible for the kids in my classes to have any separation. I probably won't change it now, but I am thinking of it for next year. But I really don't like rows.

The other thing is the seating chart. I allowed the kids to sit where they wanted in the beginning of the semester so I could get the chart set, and after that, there have been some day-to-day moves depending on problems which have come up. Next year I think I will create a seating chart based on the alphabet or some other random method. The reason would be that it would cut down, at least in the beginning of the semester, on the temptation to talk to your neighbor, because arguably this method may result in having kids sit next to someone who is not their best friend. Also, and much more importantly, it will cause them to meet someone they may not have otherwise met, or talked with much. One of my regrets, looking back at my high school experience, is the fact that I didn't meet and become friends with kids in all the different groups. I guess that's an eternal problem that won't be solved with a seating chart, but I don't want to be part of fostering that problem.

Friday. During lunch the principal mentioned that he needed to do his spring evaluation of me some time soon, meaning maybe sometime next week. I said, "How about 6th period today?" My reasons for inviting him to that class were: In history we are starting a new section, and we had pretty good discussions in 1st and 3rd periods; in his fall evaluation he didn't do this class, so he'd see a different group; and I wanted to get the formal evaluations behind me, and maybe he would, too. It's not that I mind being observed, but you do, for some reason, feel it. He pops in from time to time (two times in the past two days) for a brief look and see, and I think that's great. I know he's involved, the kids know he's involved, and it helps everyone. Anyway, the class he observed went fine, but a couple of key people were absent. The discussion would have been livelier had they been there. There was also the problem of the two or three kids in the outer row who did not participate. It's my job to get them in, and I tried, but was basically unsuccessful.

In Math, the class was more in control because of a key person being absent. It's amazing how that makes a difference. It was a pleasure going over the quiz on which the kids did pretty well. We are coming near the end of the book, so I've decided we're going to go back to the beginning and review some terms that we really didn't focus on as much as we should have. Hidden motive: I'd hate to run out of text before I run out of semester.

Well, that's it for this week, and it was a great week. Even though the changes are subtle and may not be noticeable to the casual observer, I took more control, and made the decision to be willing to do so even more in the future. That will make my job easier. There are some good ideas for next year coming out of my experiences. The beat goes on. And next week we'll be in May. Wow.

🖉 32nd Week: May 3rd - 7th

An unloaded gun was found in a locker today. Something about a trade for a pair of tennis shoes. An administrator commented that it wasn't long ago that they used to trade baseball cards.

Monday. Yesterday I put in about seven hours correcting papers and getting my grade disk up to date. The next report card grades are due in a week, and I intend to have them in by Thursday.

My history and law classes were exceptionally attentive today. I mentioned this to a veteran in a different department, and he said Mondays are like that. He was serious. The kids are tired, and not quite yet getting excited about the upcoming weekend. I hadn't paid attention to that, but in hindsight, I don't remember anything to disprove that thinking. Sounds reasonable to me. By Tuesday they start getting antsy again.

One troubled student told me he was leaving, moving out of state in a few days. I looked back over my time with this student and remembered that I hadn't been nearly as encouraging and helpful as I could have been. It made me remember that, as a teacher, I have an opportunity to do some good, so I should do it.

I talked with a parent regarding her child's grades, which are not good. The student also works and has two hobbies which are time consuming. I'll talk with him some more. The refreshing thing is that there is someone at home who cares.

I took the offensive today. I actually used my position with boldness a couple times, in positive ways, such as helping someone or cutting through some junk with a kid. He wanted me to approve of his non-performance because of his particular situation. What I gave him was advice and encouragement regarding accountability and it's consequences.

Tuesday. Today the student who is leaving turned in his book. We discussed his grade. It hit me that I didn't cut through or try to ease the anger and resentment he has because of all the lousy cards he's been dealt. All I did was do my basic job and succeed at not getting angry when he presented some discipline situations. I didn't take advantage of my opportunities to be as encouraging as I could have been.

I had my follow-up interview with my principal, following his formal evaluation. As before, he was very kind and complimentary, though I was surprised at the detailed notes he kept on his visit to my room last week. He did have some ideas on where I could improve: Occasionally I could put the desks in a full circle, seminar style, when it's a small class. Also, I could move around the room more. And the room is a mess from clutter that pre-dated me. I realize that the time has long passed when I should have had it cleaned up. The administration is going to try to find storage for it. All in all, the principal and I had a positive discussion.

An interesting side issue we discussed was dress code. I don't wear a tie but think I will in the future. About one-half of the male faculty do. For some reason, I feel as I start filling out in the role of a teacher, I'll do a better job if I treat the whole thing with a bit more respect. Many will say that's absurd, that dress has nothing to do with performance. I would've been the first to agree, and in fact there are days I wish I could wear Bermudas, but at least for me, I think I do better work if I dress for it. The kids may perceive me a little differently, more like a teacher than a buddy, and I think that's appropriate, so long as I don't walk away from moments where a kid needs a friend.

I spent a good deal of time going over the grade sheets on the back wall, re-explaining to the students how to spot their scores and to determine where they need to make up work. I explained that make-ups are due tomorrow if they want them to go on this advisory grading period report card. Kids do start to scramble over grades — in some cases, driving and dating and other privileges hang in the balance.

Wednesday. One of my teen law students asked me about a "hypothetical" case dealing with contract formation, the area we are covering now. I gave a reasonable analysis of the problem, thinking I was teaching. Turns out the student was describing a problem with a different teacher. Oops. Later, the teacher came to my room, and we discussed what was going on. No problems or animosity, just a mutual discussion about the pitfalls teachers can run into when dealing with students.

In Math, I "gave in" and told them I'd grade their paper on today's assignment. Sure enough, they all got 10s. That's fine, but I needed to make sure they also understood the problems.

There was a snake show in the library today. I didn't know about it or I would've arranged for my wife and kids to see it. I guess the point is to be aware of what's going on.

I did a good exercise in Teen Law today. I had them write directions to a space alien as to how to put on and tie a shoe. One student would have to follow another student's directions literally. There were some pretty funny results. We are in a unit on contract formation, and the point is how difficult it is to write a concise sentence.

Thursday. One very quiet student had a birthday today. Earlier in the year, for a more vocal and assertive student's birthday, we sang and had a cake. Today we did nothing. I thought, the student didn't want class involvement in his life, so I didn't intrude. Right or wrong?

I gave tests in Math and History. The math class had their choruses of, "We never went over this," and, "This is stupid." It was a very stark contrast going from that, to the next period, which is a good history class.

I stayed late after class and was up last night previewing a movie, *The Grapes of Wrath*. I have four pages of questions for the kids to answer as they are watching. I think it's generally not real effective to just show a movie unless the students have some immediate need to pay attention.

Friday. I just got home from a play put on by the drama club — a musical, and it was great. The young women all had professional-sounding voices, and there were some mature topics explored, such as getting "the curse," choosing a mate, getting married, having kids and dying. It was a stark contrast to what I see in the kids around the halls during the day. I'm constantly amazed at what the kids do in their extracurricular times. There may be a huge lesson there regarding getting the kids to also see the fun or relevancy of what they are doing in their school work. That component is built into extracurricular activities they choose, and look at their effort.

Today, a student was mentioning how a certain teacher is a "no-nonsense" teacher, and another jumped in and said he's a stud. No doubt in my mind, that the tougher the teacher, the more he is respected, so long as he is fair and consistent.

I spent some time today thinking about things I need to order or type or copy for the first few weeks of next year. One will be a revised set of class rules. It will be much more comprehensive, a bit stricter, and enough said. You can't legislate morality, but in school, I think you can legislate an atmosphere that is conducive to learning.

✒ 33rd Week: May 10th - 14th

Another thing I've realized, and this is major: It's not my duty to entertain the kids each day. Yes, I try to have fun and make it interesting, but I'm not going to kill myself if my class is a bit dry sometimes. They need to go to work, too. I think having that attitude will actually result in being a better teacher, because I'm not laboring under undue pressure all the time.

Monday. Today was a bit of a nothing day. I'm continuing to show *The Grapes of Wrath* in my three history classes, and I'm showing *Stand and Deliver* in my math class. These are both great movies, loaded with things to talk about with the kids. And during the four hours of movies, I got caught up in History, getting the next chapters outlined with an idea as to how I want to proceed.

I catch myself thinking of changes I'll make next year, and one thing I'll do is show *Stand and Deliver* early on to all my classes. My purpose will be to inspire maybe a student or two, and definitely to inspire myself. This year I've been on the defensive, trying to survive and make no major mistakes. I think that's normal and even reasonable for a first-year teacher. But next year I'll be willing to act like I know more about what I'll expect — no, require — of the kids. They'll rise or sink to the level of my expectations, and those will be higher next year in terms of academics and behavior.

I went through more of my room and cleaned out stuff. I've got the janitors, my department head and the facilities director involved now, so finally I must mean business. The teacher who used to be in there has been notified of the clean-out, so I'll have a clear conscience making a fairly clean sweep. I spent about four hours Sunday in the room boxing stuff up, and previewing this week's lessons.

Tuesday. 1st period gave me a pleasant surprise. We finished watching *The Grapes of Wrath*. On the work sheet I had given them, there were some questions regarding dignity, homelessness and prejudice. The last few scenes of the movie are grabbers, and can cause you to get a bit emotional if you are so inclined. Well, at the end of the movie, the room was totally quiet, and it stayed that way for about three minutes. I was amazed and impressed. 3rd and 6th periods did not have the same reaction, but we'll go over the movie and questions tomorrow and see if they catch on.

I gave a test in Teen Law. One fairly good student who is sluffing off asked a question I've heard a bit lately, "Mr. Gish, if I have a B- now and flunk this test, what will I have?" At least there was some honesty there, as he starts mapping his strategy for the rest of the semester.

There was an assembly in the middle of the day. I don't feel bad saying that it was a waste of time. At least that's what the students and faculty that I heard said. I think the idea of letting the kids have some fun is fine, but for some reason, those assemblies don't seem to accomplish that, or anything else. It's like we're waiting for something to go wrong, such as a fight or a huge social blunder or something, and when it's over, we're relieved when it didn't.

There are some special ed. kids throughout the school, and at the assembly, one section of kids cheered too loud and too long when a special ed. kid walked on the floor to try to participate. It was abusive and ugly. One of the teachers said he was going to talk to the administration about it. Where do we start with manners and compassion?

We had a department meeting. Very short. One teacher is going on a book-buying trip and wanted input. Also, an issue about portables being placed on campus next year was discussed. I still like my idea of putting them in front of the school, right by the main street, so the voters can see what's going on. Don't hide them in back, as is planned.

I don't know when it happened, but it did. I've definitely taken a turn for the stricter, and I like it. My standard answer now, when someone asks to leave the room during class, is "No." It used to be "Yes." I always assumed students had a legitimate problem that needed to be taken care of right away. They usually didn't. Funny thing is, kids just accept the "no" and go back to their seats, no harm, no foul. And it makes for a better class.

Another thing I've realized, and this is major: It's not my duty to entertain the kids each day. Yes, I try to have fun and make it interesting, but I'm not going to kill myself if my class is a bit dry sometimes. They need to go to work, too. I think having that attitude will actually result in being a better teacher, because I'm not laboring under undue pressure all the time.

The room muck-out has continued. It will be cleaned by the end of the week. From the many times I've referred to this problem, it sounds like this place must've been a land-fill. No, I've just been slow and cautious about what to get rid of.

Wednesday. I had the best class of the year today, and here's what happened: It was 6th period History. We are in between units, having finished the New Deal and getting ready for World War II, but the kids didn't know that. We had a serious discussion about *The Grapes of Wrath* and the issues of prejudice, homelessness, economic possibilities, desperation, dignity, and so on. In the middle of the discussion, I moved one chatty girl. The room became very quiet for two reasons: First, I made the discipline move, and that lets everyone know that Mr. Gish isn't tolerating as much as he sometimes does, and second, the subject matter was heavy. Then, when we finished that, I moved the discussion to talking about something that was in the news lately, which was a religious cult. We talked about why people join them, whether or not they are satisfied with their life, and the freedoms they give up by giving allegiance to someone. The kids really got into it and argued about those points. At the end, I told them that we weren't just talking about a recent cult leader, but also about Hitler, and welcome to World War II. They enjoyed it a lot, and frankly, so did I.

In law we are getting ready for the trip to the Supreme Court. I do have two guest students from another class who also want to go. They were in class today to get the material, and I was a bit embarrassed. It was a loud day because the kids were working together in groups briefing and discussing the cases. Tomorrow will have more structure, because I have prepared a brief sheet for the kids to fill out for each case that will help this adventure work.

In Math, we finished *Stand and Deliver*, and right at the end, everyone said how great it was. Then, for the last few minutes of class, they went right back to their unfortunate little gossipy discussions. It was partly my fault for not being aggressive enough to dive into a longer discussion about pride and performance.

Thursday. I think I learned a good thing today. My best days are when I do what I want to do. My worst days are when I let the kids talk me into doing less than I planned. And they try that just about daily. Have a plan, stick to it, and try to use the 55 minutes. I need to get better at that.

In getting ready for the Supreme Court I am not as organized as I'd like it to be. Tomorrow we'll go over the four cases in small groups, to make sure everyone has them basically understood. I won't feel bad if it's not perfectly orchestrated, because it is an innovative stretch, and I'd rather do these things knowing they won't be perfect than avoid doing them because they're too much work. I do wonder how many will actually show up at 5:45 a.m. on Tuesday. I hope I do.

A bit of excitement on campus today. There is a convention of transvestites in town, and, by invitation, a couple of them came to a Sociology class to speak. It caused a stir on campus, with some ugly threats involved.

The test for Advanced Placement U.S. History, which I don't teach, was today. One student who took the test at a different school came to visit a friend in my class in 6th period. I talked with him about how his A.P. teacher taught the class, thinking someone must have some golden ideas of innovation. Nope. Mostly lecture with worksheets, and the added homework you'd expect in an A.P. class.

It feels great being in a classroom that looks like a classroom instead of a bad warehouse. I'm still not done getting rid of outdated stuff, but the major work has been done. Now, to clean up my desk area. I've got no excuses on that one.

I had a heart-to-heart talk with one student who is flunking. I've been talking to him along the way, but today we got serious. He's not (much of) a class disturbance, and sometimes appears to be doing his work and joins in the talks. I told him it's not up to me to keep pushing him, it's up to him to get the stuff done. If not, he's wasting his time. It's his choice.

I had my second student in after school because of tardiness to class. I'm not sure it has much of an effect, but at least they see I'm following through on my tardy policy.

Friday. I was a better teacher today. More control over the room, calling on people randomly to keep all of them on their toes. It's so obvious, but it works. In History we started in on Adolph Hitler, and had good discussions about how a tyrant gets power, and what to look for. It just happened to be on the day *Channel One* opened with a quote from Thomas Jefferson about having a free press as the safeguard of a society.

The student newspaper was delivered while I made a quick run to the library. The kids immediately began to look at that instead of finishing their assignment. I got them a bit back on track, but that was unfortunate timing. Or, I shouldn't have left the room.

I subbed during my planning period in the science building. I don't know much (anything?) about the equipment there, so after one kid did an experiment with an electric shock ball and got shocked (like he is supposed to), I told the kids that all the equipment was off limits for the day. They obeyed, but later I heard that the piece of equipment the kids were using didn't work. I'll have to find out what happened.

I had an errand at lunch and left my history notebook in the car when I came back to class. I realized that at the start of 6th period, but went ahead with the lecture without benefit of the notebook. That could be a sign of getting better as a teacher, but the truth is, I had most of the important notes already on the overhead from the earlier periods.

There was a track meet after school in which I, and about 30 other teachers, helped. I had a good discussion about the teaching profession with a veteran coach I was paired with. One point he made was the kids are really getting antsy this time of year. He also told me that he made a comment about one student which was construed the wrong way. You've got to be careful what you say. And many teachers would be quick to point out that the students do not need to be careful what they say.

✏ 34th Week: May 17th - 21st

It seems a day doesn't go by anymore that I don't move someone. My toleration level is lower, and the result is I'm gaining better control of the classroom. The kids know it, more is getting done, and we all like it better.

Monday. This was a weird weekend. I went back to my home-town area to see some friends and to drop my oldest son to stay overnight with a friend. I began wondering if I want to stay here next year or look for a job back near my hometown. That's not really part of the journal, but I wonder if my attitude of uncertainty will affect how I see my job.

Sunday I spent about three hours correcting papers and getting my grade book caught up.

I'll be gone tomorrow on the field trip to the state Supreme Court from 6:00 a.m. to 6:00 p.m. I had to get the room ready for the sub, and that went well. I'll have my history classes doing a map assignment, Math doing the next assignment, and the law students who are not going on the field trip doing a few assignments out of the old text. All is set and should go well. The room looks much better, so I feel good about having a sub come in.

The kids were all kind of quiet today. I guess the "tired Monday" idea really is true. It's too far away from the next weekend for them to be getting antsy.

Today (May 17th) was the first real day of spring, and though the weather didn't affect attitudes much today, I think it will in the future. The busier I keep them, the less that kind of stuff will matter.

Tuesday. Field trip. Only 13 students went. Many in the class ended up not going because they didn't want or weren't allowed to miss any more school. This is too late in the year to take a field trip.

Those who went were a good group of kids. We got to the court on time, after about a three-hour bus ride, which included a stop alongside the road so a couple of the guys could relieve themselves. There's nothing in the field trip manual about that.

It was a very interesting day at the Supreme Court, including hearing three cases and getting a behind-the-scenes tour by one of the

Justices. That was a rare treat, touring in and out of the offices where the Justices work, and the kids seem to realize and appreciate that.

The Justice who gave us the private tour was recently elected. She is fairly young, as far as Supreme Court justices go. In fact, she and I graduated from law school in the same year, and I couldn't help but dwell a bit on the divergent courses our careers have taken. One of the treats was having her admit that one of the morning cases was quite boring. That honesty won her some points with the students.

The bus driver is the mom of one of my students, whose grade is, well let's just say it's in the Southern Hemisphere. We talked about that — she is very concerned, and she will try to get him motivated.

When I got back to campus, I checked my room. Four of the five classes went well. My math class had a few screw-ups, and I'll address that tomorrow. It's embarrassing to me when a sub comes in and has trouble. Nothing major, just general impoliteness. But it's not acceptable, and I will talk with the offenders tomorrow.

Wednesday and Thursday. I talked with the kids the substitute identified as being rude, and wanted them to know that their behavior isn't unnoticed. They could tell I was upset, and I wanted to present the whole thing to them in a way that would be meaningful to them, not just sound preachy. I challenged them to try to be polite for 24 hours, even when those around them aren't. We'll see.

In History we blitzed through the highlights of World War II. We all worked hard. After class, as the kids were filing out, they looked drained. It was a good feeling and reminded me of a basketball turn-out where everyone worked hard and had a sense of pride in what was done. We need more of that. I won't allow myself to think of the possibility that maybe they were just sleepy.

Today, three computers got delivered to our department, and I'll get one of them. It's in my room in boxes, waiting for me to arrange the tables so the computer guy can come and set it up. Most of us in the Social Studies department now have our own computer. Wow, that's a nice set-up. I'll probably be in the room about 6:00 tomorrow morning to get the room ready, because I want it to get set up. The room has seen too many boxes piled up as it is.

I got called up to the basketball coaches room to sub a few minutes while he went to a meeting. We went over the summer schedule for the basketball program. Our teams will be involved in several camps and two summer leagues. Very busy. I'm not sure what my availability will be.

This is a big personal issue and may or may not end up being relevant for this journal, but it's part of my year and therefore belongs in here: I called a teacher I know in a different district to get some answers about how I go about letting people around here know I am applying for a different teaching job. I still feel iffy about it, but today I sent in my application letter to a different district. I'm weighing heavily who I would approach around here to get a letter of recommendation, without looking like I'm a traitor. The veteran teacher I talked with said it's no problem. There is much movement in the teaching profession, and everyone knows it. I talked with another who said her teacher-husband once moved after one year in a district. I guess it happens, but it still doesn't feel right. However, I am excited about the new possibility. It has nothing to do with anything negative in my current setting. It's just that the move would put us close to my aging parents, my long-term friends (like me, also aging) and other hometown attractions.

Thursday in History was a bit of a waste. I had promised the kids a movie, so I used one recommended by a veteran teacher. It was okay in the beginning, but got old. Lesson: Never show a movie until you've looked at it through the eyes of a mildly bored student, and almost never unless you've got a question sheet to be answered along the way. Again, unless the kids are going to be held accountable for it, they don't have a lot of incentive to do much.

Friday. Today was something called, "Senior slave day." Seniors were put on the auction block a week or so ago, and the bidders bid cans of food for the food bank. When you were top bidder, you owned that Senior for the day, and could make them wear goofy clothes and do menial tasks for you. It was a bit weird, but entertaining.

Yesterday, outside of the main office, three guys from the band did an impromptu number with their drum sticks on a handrail, garbage can and metal post. Very loud, possibly damaging to some property, but not bad. It drew a lot of attention, and no one thought of stopping them. I admit my toe was tapping.

Today one of my students rushed up to me between periods and said, "Mr. Gish, there's a rubber on your doorknob!" She was right. I took it off, was thankful that it was "clean," and asked a few kids some questions, but got nowhere. I have no suspects, and as I write tonight,

I realize I should've told our discipline vice-principal about it. For some reason it sort of hit me as someone's idea of a Friday prank, and I wasn't real affected by it. Either I'm getting numb or lazy. I guess it was also sick and disgusting. I'll make the report Monday.

In History, I was a bit amazed. I've found that if I start into a lecture, with discussion questions aimed at students at random, the class listens. You never know when you're going to get "picked on." Get into a couple of controversial issues and the class comes alive. Also, one trick lately is that I've turned off the classroom lights. There's a big wall window, so it's still quite light in the room, but it causes the class to focus on the overhead screen and seems to promote a quieter atmosphere. 1st and 3rd periods were fine, but 6th period was a bit rowdy.

It's no surprise and probably too obvious to bear repeating, but the busier you and the students are, the faster the time passes. I'm finding that lately, as I'm using more of the class hour and encouraging more attention by moving loud students, the more gets done. The better it is for everyone. It's a win-win situation.

I had bus duty again this week, and it was uneventful. I guess that's good. One kid tried to make a field goal over the telephone wire with a pop can. I saw the last bit of it, and told him to pick it up. Incidently, the kick was low.

The big new issue in my life continues to linger. I have applied for a job back in my home area. I'm not totally qualified for it because the position mentions a Social Studies and English endorsement is preferred, or Basketball coaching ability. I fit about one and one-half of those categories. I suppose if the situation were right, and all they needed was an assistant basketball coach and maybe only a filler for English (like I'm doing this year in Math), it could work. But I remain torn about the whole thing. I haven't mentioned it to anyone around here, which I obviously would need to do in order to get some current recommendations. There are several people I could approach, and I'm sure they'd be glad to help, but I don't feel like making my possible move public. I think I'm waiting to see if I get called for an interview. Then I'll know they are serious, and I won't have spilled my beans for nothing.

It's a gut wrencher.

✎35th Week: May 24th - 28th

I realized that now, eight months into this year, I was not thinking about time in terms of normal humans — I was thinking in terms of periods. My guest was talking one o'clock, I was talking 5th period.

Monday. This weekend I was weighed down with the thought about applying for the other job. I guess an even heavier question could be faced by someone who is finishing their first year and wondering if they want to teach anymore.

In History, we've been in World War II longer than I thought. I tried to reserve the library for my classes for two days, but it's booked up. I'll take two days next week instead. It would have been better if I had reserved the correct days ahead of time, but my guess is that no matter how many years of experience you have, you won't always be able to plan perfectly.

I posted updated grades today. I had to be ready for all the complaints and questions about grades I may've put down wrong, or from kids who want to make up zeroes or poor grades.

In one period, one of my best students talked to me quite frankly about the teaching profession. This student should be in the A.P. class, and agreed with me on that point. She thought I was too lax on some people and gave too many extra chances for some and too much work time in class. We talked about how almost everyone in class has jobs, which makes it hard to do homework. Anticipating the performance capabilities of the students has been a guess. If anything, I've guessed too low. I agreed that I am a bit too lax, but things are changing.

I created the History test for Wednesday. It's a bit tougher than I thought it would be, but it's a good test. I'll warn them tomorrow, and see how they do.

I've still taken to having the lights off during lecture/discussion. Today it was 80 degrees, and I'm on the sunny side of the building. I think there's a psychological coolness if the lights are off. The kids focus better, chatting is about nil, and the whole thing seems more interesting. I can think of some rooms where lights off would cause things to get too interesting, however.

I've got about three weeks left, and, this will sound weird, but I wish there were more time. I want to cover things in history and law that I won't have time for.

Tuesday. I went to the library first thing and got Wednesday's test copied and ready to go. That seemed to make today easier, knowing I'm ready for Wednesday.

I had a basketball meeting today, and went over the summer schedule of camps and various league games. It's very busy and basically a year-round job for the head coach. I'll not be that involved this year. I have too much stuff to do around our unfinished house and with the family, including our month-long camping trip to and from Disneyland. How do you spell "A-m-e-r-i-c-a-n-a?"

One veteran came to my room regarding a video stolen from his desk. We had a brief discussion about the lack of security around here. We especially noted the new computers and printers which are just sitting on the desks. I'm pleasantly surprised that nothing has been swiped from my room yet, though I do generally lock up my notebooks in the filing cabinet.

I warned all my history students today to study their notes ahead of time, that I won't be giving any extra time to work on the test. It will be interesting to see how many want more time or will somehow complain about the test. It won't be the A students, but if it is, then I'll re-check my thinking on the whole deal.

Wednesday. I gave the test in History today. Yes, a few of the kids complained about not having enough time, but most finished well in time. It's still a relief when the first few have turned it in, and you see that it actually made sense.

One of my students got pictures developed from her trip to Europe last summer and shared them with me before school. That was a nice gesture, and they were great pictures. We, or she, decided against handing them around to the class. The chance of them getting smudged or otherwise damaged outweighed any real benefit the class would have received.

I went to the courthouse during my planning period. I was going to talk to the Family Law judge, but he was busy. I did see another person, whom I later called to be a guest speaker. I realized that now, eight months into this year, I was not thinking about time in terms of normal humans, I was thinking in terms of periods. My guest was talking one o'clock, I was talking 5th period. But it worked, and he'll be in in a week or so.

One thing that hasn't come through in this journal is the relationship that develops with the classes. It is subtle, but nice. I will miss
some of the kids, and I will be interested in how all of them do. I'm
beginning to think in terms of a last-day party or toast or something.
On that score, I had a note sent to one of my basketball players wish-
ing him well in a spring event in which he is competing at "state." I
feel somehow connected.

An administrator talked with me about his hometown, indicating he
may be retiring in a couple years and moving back there. He made it
sound so easy. I'm wrestling harder with the application I put in at the
other school.

Thursday. I am ready for the next six days of my history classes.
We'll spend most of that time on a movie, and two days in the library
working on World War II reports.

I can imagine a veteran reading that and laughing over a rookie's
happiness about being one week ahead. I assume many veterans have
the whole year mapped out in advance, although come to think of it, I
don't think that would be possible because of updates, changes, and
in-class variations that may dictate an unexpected pace.

I thought about having the A and B students exempted from answering the questions on the movie we're watching. Nope, I didn't do
it. I'll include information from this movie on the next test, and it'd
be unfair if they didn't have the notes to study. It would be, however,
a good lesson on discrimination of the appropriate kind — the movie,
Separate But Equal, is about inappropriate discrimination. The kids
will learn that they are going to be discriminated against according to
how they perform in life.

You gotta have thick skin. I did a good job of holding my temper
when one kid really bugged me by his slight sassiness. Just a glare,
and a count to five, and I was back in the game. I've got to remember
that even if I'm doing something wonderful, some kids will be on
their own page, so I can't take negative reactions personally.

Two nights this week I was up till midnight watching the movie I'll
be showing, and preparing questions for the kids to answer as they
watch. Then I was at the library when it opened at 7:00 a.m. I need to
make sure I get things copied in time for first period.

There was a career fair in the student center, and classes were invited to attend. Naturally, my classes pressured me to attend, but I
didn't. It's clear that from the beginning of the year, my concern about

students' reaction to that type of decision has been reduced. After a couple of groans, we all get down to the business at hand.

I received a nice compliment. It appears I'll be teaching one period of Contemporary Issues, a Senior class. A few of my Juniors in history were chatting, not for my benefit, about trying to arrange their schedule so they can get in my class. Nice feeling. Of course, maybe they want me because they can spot an easy mark.

Friday. We continued with the movie and questions. Some kids commented it was a good movie, and some thought otherwise. One student, a good student, said the movie was aggravating because he didn't like the prejudice that the movie portrays. He is definitely tuned in, and that is most of the victory.

I subbed during my planning period. This time, auto mechanics. It was a useful period — I think I found someone to fix my lawn mower.

I received my final evaluation from my principal. The categories covered: Professional Preparation and Scholarship, Knowledge of Subject Matter, Instructional Skills, Classroom Management, Handling of Student Discipline and Attendance Problems, Interest in Teaching Pupils, Effort Towards Improvement When Needed, and Additional Comments. It was very glowing, and I'm a bit embarrassed because I don't feel I deserve his high praise. Next year, I'll come closer to earning the nice comments he made.

Now for the goofy part. Right after the day ended, I called the place I have applied for work and faxed them a copy of the evaluation. I've been assured by the veterans I've talked to that applying somewhere else is totally reasonable. But I feel funny using my principal's report to try to get a job somewhere else, which will result in his having to do more work, such as screening and interviewing. By early next week we'll know if that's an issue.

The rest of the year, which consists of about two weeks, is going to be a bit of a reward time for the kids. We'll be hitting some major topics without much time to deal with detail. We'll have some movie time, the library report, some guest speakers, and that'll be it.

I still need to do the "Bronx Connection" video. I've got to get it done next week and in the mail. I talked with the video class and have arranged to borrow a video recorder.

✐ 36th Week: Jun. 1st - 4th

I need to remind myself to keep a thick skin and not to notice everything that happens.

Tuesday, June 1st. In History, we are in the library for two days, doing reports on World War II. I attempt to be fairly active on these report projects, and not just use the time in the library as slack time.

In Law, we are finishing up the movie *Separate But Equal*. I got a call from a local judge who agreed to be a guest speaker this Thursday. The other guest speaker will be the following Thursday, so I guess that's good spacing. In Math we are continuing in Chapter 16, which is the last chapter in the book.

I began filming today for the "Bronx Video." The kids are real curious about what's going on as I walk into the lunchroom or down a hallway with the camera running. Most are willing to get on the air and say something, though. It'll continue tomorrow and Thursday. I've got to get it in the mail by Thursday, and it'll be late even at that.

Today was the first day of basketball camp, a one-week deal to get the kids ready for the summer leagues. It really is a year-round job for the varsity coach. I won't have time to be as involved as I probably should be.

I talked with the student who is taking my history class by independent study. She's fallen behind, but is going to catch up. Her counselor and I are both disappointed in her lack of follow through, and agreed it is an experiment that won't happen again.

I heard today that I am not a candidate for the other job I was looking at. I would have needed an endorsement in English in order to be considered. My reaction is mixed — some disappointment, but some relief now that the issue is behind us. On with the year.

This evening, we had a fellow teacher and his wife over for dinner. We talked about our jobs and many other things. He's a bit frustrated about being led to believe he had an assistant-coaching job which was taken from him at the last minute. He mentioned his possible willingness to start looking soon for a different position. I mentioned my desire to be near my home area. It is a fluid profession, I keep rationalizing. I confided my situation to one veteran, who told me, if the administration wants to prevent movement, they could offer people contracts of more than just one year. Frankly, I don't think that would really matter, because some people leave, with administrative permission, even after signing a contract for the next year. It probably depends on where you are, but our administration is very cooperative and supportive.

I had a discussion with a veteran about how to construct tests. A multiple-choice question is where you just allow the student to complete the sentence by selecting from the choices available. A good multiple-choice question is tough to devise, and to be effective requires that there has been critical teaching going on. I'm afraid much of my teaching is too vague and concept-oriented to allow for good multiple-choice questions. I need to tighten things a bit for that.

Also, every time you give a test you assume some students will complain about any given question, so you have to be able to justify them all. Another teacher mentioned that he, on occasion, has had a student who is critical of a certain question try to compose the challenged question to their satisfaction. He's found that they usually realize that almost any form is open for criticism.

Wednesday. Today, unfortunately before classes, they passed out the yearbooks. Guess what the students were looking at all day? An easy fix is to wait until about the last day of the year, and hand them out the last hour of that date. Or, I could simply make a rule that they keep them put away or else, lose them.

Another distraction today was the spring blood drive. Kids were coming and going all day.

I continued making the video that is going to the high school in New York City. I think I made a bit of a nuisance of myself, but I got a lot of scenes with students, faculty and administrators. I have to get that off in the mail tomorrow.

We had basketball "camp" today after school. About 45 hopefuls for next year.

I've enjoyed being prepared ahead of time, even though to a large extent it involves library and video assignments. My evenings are much more relaxed. I anticipate that will translate into better preparation in regular lesson plans next year. I catch myself thinking about the first few weeks of next year.

Good, bad or otherwise, I've found myself acting a bit like a "veteran." As an example, for this video I'm sending to New York, I find myself barging into colleagues' classrooms with the video camera running. That is not something I would have done the first few months of school. I'm worrying less about what people might think about what I do, and worried more about just doing a good, aggressive job of what I want to do. From defensive to offensive. I guess that's what June 2nd will do for you.

Thursday. In Law, I had a guest speaker, a local judge. He was well-received by the students and had an easy manner of dealing with them. They liked him. Also, his talk about the adversarial environment he is involved in vividly took me back to my law career days and confirmed my decision to get into teaching and coaching.

There was one student who was not paying attention. I pointed him out by name, and he didn't like that. I later talked to him about not being rude to a guest speaker. He said I handled it wrong, and he would've done it differently. Maybe he's right.

Friday. The movie continued in History. I still think it's a great movie, though I suppose I'm open to the charge of having a "plan in a can" because of the number of video days lately. I plan on developing a summary of the movie and handing it out for a discussion guide after it is over on Monday.

I was critical of one of the Senior boys today. He did something immature, and I accused him of acting like a Sophomore, sort of jokingly. He wasn't amused, but I didn't back down. Nothing came of it, and we wished each other a nice weekend, but I seem to be doing a bit more of that lately. I need to remind myself to keep a thick skin and not to notice everything that happens.

I was late to school this morning, meaning I was only 20 minutes early for the first class. A worker from the kitchen was wandering around campus offering cinnamon rolls, and since I was too late for a breakfast at home, I jumped at the offer. She also thanked me for putting up with all the bad attitudes and actions of the kids this year. I don't recall ever being treated badly, but I knew what she meant.

The Seniors are graduating next week, and it's starting to be time to reminisce over their 12 or 13 years of school. I feel like a newcomer, though the kids are saying nice stuff about me as they compare me to other teachers they've had through the years.

I was thinking today I want to get a big T-shirt and have all my students sign it. Is that weird? I also am thinking of a way to tell them about this journal. After all, the kids have a big role in this.

I have played golf the last couple of Fridays with several of the staff from school. That's been fun, though I wish that sort of stuff had gone on more, earlier. It's a matter of just doing it, I guess. But it does take time away from the family. There's a balance in there somewhere.

I'm re-thinking my seating arrangement for next year. I had become convinced that I would use conventional rows. That would hold down the chattiness that goes on if the seats are in a U-shape, because in that arrangement the desks touch each other. I'm now thinking I'll leave it a U-shape, and simply control what goes on more, and be quick to move offenders around.

Only about two weeks to go.

✏ 37th Week: Jun. 7th - 11th

It is tempting to think about coasting. But I remember, like on the first day in September, when the bell rings on Monday, there will be 30 or so kids waiting for my plan and supporting brilliance. Coasting isn't an option. I've got to keep getting ready. The treadmill continues.

Monday. It's getting close to the end, and the kids are acting accordingly. The Seniors graduate this Friday night, and Wednesday is their last real day of school. I'll be giving tests on Wednesday for the few Seniors I have.

My theory is the busier we are, the faster the time will fly. My theory is right, but my actions don't always follow my intentions.

The Superintendent of the school district walked in during History. We were having a discussion on the Cold War and the policy of containment. It was a lively discussion with good, opposing ideas about the United States' role in world affairs being offered vigorously. He was enjoying and even participating in the discussion, and said something to the effect that it was a very interesting time, and he wished he could do this all day. That made my morning. One positive thing I noticed was that the discussion and the attitudes of the kids and I really didn't change after he walked in. After he left, however, I did resume breathing.

It's an interesting time in my history classes. I only have seven days of teaching left, and about a million topics I could cover. In their Senior year, the kids will take Contemporary Issues, which I'm tempted to get into right now. Next year in history I will spend much less time on certain areas to have more time to deal with current issues. Frankly, it's easier and therefore more fun to teach. It's also interesting to the kids to tie in past events as causation for events we are studying now. Next year, I'll obviously know more content, and be ready to use and take advantage of those lead-ins.

I have not planned my Law semester as well as I could have. I'll be giving a test Wednesday on Family Law, and after that, we'll have about four days of teaching prior to the final test day. I'll do a bit from various topics that the kids have expressed interest in over the semester, but I won't pretend that it will flow very smoothly.

Tuesday. I'm very tired. Not much sleep last night, but the show must go on. We had a department meeting today and discussed the pilot textbooks we would be using next year. All are very nice, comprehensive, colorful, expensive, and will be completely out-dated in five years. But that's another story.

I brought up that I'd like it mentioned to the administration that yearbooks shouldn't be distributed so soon. The teachers told me they simply tell the kids that if they see them out during class, they will be confiscated. I haven't been that tough, but that's a perfect example of how a rookie needs to grow. Get tough, be consistent, and the kids will respect you, and you'll get more done in class.

I am doing some year-end housecleaning in History, and it's not as organized as it could be. But I am hitting some important stuff, and am at least even with the other teachers.

Wednesday. There was a faculty meeting after school. It wasn't the regular type of meeting, because the main purpose was to give a farewell to three retiring teachers. It was fun and funny, because more than a few jokes were thrown around at the expense of the retirees.

I covered Vietnam in class today. Obviously, I did a very surface job, hitting the chronological highlights. Actually, I was looking through one of the text-books we'll be using next year, and it had a lot more on Vietnam than our current text. I discovered a one-page chronology and hurriedly copied it for my three classes. I probably broke a copyright law or two, come to think of it.

I also hit JFK, LBJ, McArthyism, and 1968 in the same hour. The reason that sounds absurd is because it is. What I have determined is that next year I'll take about the first eight chapters of the book, regarding the discovery of our continent, and combine them into about a two-week lesson, thus freeing up a month or more at this end of the year. Other places during the year I'll do the same.

Thursday. Today was the last day for the Seniors, and it was a half-day at that. I got to school early and went to the cafeteria for a cup of coffee. What really happened is that I got drafted to help serve at the Senior Breakfast. The most popular item was coffee because apparently last night there was an all-night party, or two. Most of the kids looked pretty rugged. And those were the ones who showed up.

I had a guest speaker in Law today: a local attorney who could tell a few good stories, and is very experienced. The kids were attentive. In the beginning, one kid was talking to his buddy, so I didn't mess around

171

with it, I simply motioned for him to move. He seemed surprised that I took that action, but he moved. What I was unable to do (move noisy students) with all my analysis and worry in the beginning of the year, I am now doing in a split-second with my little finger and a look. Not too cerebral, but that is progress. I guess I have thin skin when it comes to kids being rude to guest speakers.

I am preparing for the last few days of math class. We finished the book yesterday, and that could be a terrible problem. What to do? In this case, it's easy. I've got four days of class left before the test day. I'm going to go over selected vocabulary and a few highlight questions from each chapter. I'll give them a closed-book test on all this the last day. That'll be a good review.

I started showing *All The President's Men* in my history classes. There's timing and then there's timing. It just happened that in last night's local paper there was a political cartoon about Nixon being "Tanned, Rested and Ready" to help out in the Clinton Administration. I hit the copy room at about 7:15 (after the Senior Breakfast) and copied off a class set. One student mentioned she didn't understand what it was about, which of course was a perfect lead in to why they needed to know about Watergate. The movie, in spite of some bad language, shows not only the Watergate story, but also what investigative journalism can be like. The kids' complaint is that they don't know what's going on. I pointed out that neither did Woodward or Bernstein, and gave them some hints along the way to keep them on track. A modern-day Deep Throat.

A couple kids are scrambling to get enough points to get at least a D. I've given them some old work they haven't done, and we'll see if they follow through.

Getting the books checked in and signing off the Seniors was a bit weird. Nothing real emotional, just kind of a relief on their behalf — they are finally done with the warehousing they've been through. Also, in a few instances, I had a bit of regret for the things I didn't teach them.

In History I'm using the movie time to correct the teen law and math tests I just gave. The movie will go on for another day and a little, and I honestly don't know what I'll do with the last couple days. According to state law I have to spend at least one day speaking about AIDS, and that will probably be Tuesday. It's always in the news and we have dealt with various aspects of the issue from time to time, but state law says we have to spend some time on it, so I'm sneaking it in on the last day. I hope to get into morality discussions. The kids like to do that, it gets heated, and I think I have ideas which will help them.

Wednesday is the final day before the two testing days. Should I plan something special and fun? Should I tell everyone about this journal, which I hope to have turned into a book? I'll think about it.

Friday. I did something very obvious, and it worked. Maybe the things that are so obvious I miss, but here was a simple solution I picked up at the department meeting a few days ago: Some kids had their yearbooks out at the beginning of class, so I simply said that everyone needed to clear their desks. They did. No discrimination. No picking on anyone. Just a broad order.

The Watergate movie I'm showing had some timely bits in the news to go with it. Here we are, about 20 years after the event, and two things appear in the paper this week relating to Nixon and Watergate. It pays to be alert to current stuff and relate it to what's going on in class. Those news bits perked the kids' interest in the work we are doing.

The classes are smaller now that the Seniors are gone. The Underclassmen are sort of looking for leadership. I know it shouldn't be, but it is easier to run the classes without the Seniors there. They were really ready to get out of here the last few weeks, anyway.

I volunteered as an usher at the graduation ceremony. I was surprised, but they actually needed ushers to get the crowd stuffed into the seats. The gym was very crowded. There were three small, nice, speeches by graduates. A fairly uneventful ceremony. The actual diplomas are withheld until Monday, so staff can make sure the students' books and fines are taken care of, and to make sure students don't misbehave at the ceremony. The memorable part was after the ceremony out on the lawn. Many hugs and tears between kids and kids, kids and parents, kids and a few teachers and a few parents and teachers. It is the passing of a huge thing in their lives.

There was an article today in the paper about how one student at a different school, in the 11th grade, still basically can't write. A reminder that you're not doing a kid any favors to just pass him along. I know I've not been very strict about grammar and spelling in my history and law essays. I will be more so in the future.

I had a good discussion with a couple other teachers about teacher dress codes and students' foul language. Regarding the language, we agreed that something needs to be done, even though trying to enforce a rule about certain words may not be possible. We also agreed that even though there's no real reason for it, we all seem to act more professional when we dress more professional. An example of that is to observe students when they are dressed up. It is different. I will dress up a bit more often in the future, although today, in sunny June, I'm trying to figure out if I should ask the principal if I can wear shorts the last day of school. Maybe a little inconsistent?

Next week is the last week. I have Monday, Tuesday and Wednesday to teach, with testing on Thursday and Friday, and then that's basically it. It is tempting to think about coasting. But I remember, like on the first day in September, when the bell rings on Monday, there will be 30 or so kids waiting for my plan and supporting brilliance. Coasting isn't an option. I've got to keep getting ready. The treadmill continues.

✎ 38th Week: Jun. 14th - 18th

I wonder if it's hitting me, that this year is really about one day from ending, and my time with these kids will be over ... I'm wondering if I'll miss them and how I could've done a better job ...

Monday. For some reason, I'm not frantically excited about the year ending. It was a rainy day, and the hours were occupied, so it felt more like March than June. I am always getting pressure from the kids to slack off because it's the last week of school. I point out to them that the time to slack off is the week *after* the last week of school.

I'm wrestling with creating a "big finish" for the school year, and I think I'll come up empty. I may have some food in the room on the last day or something like that, but I don't have any inspired closer coming to me just yet. I am wrestling with telling them about this book, but I was hoping to deliver that news when I had a publisher and it was more or less a set deal that it would become a book of some sort. As of tonight, no bites from the many publishers I've written to.

I'm allowing my few F students to make up any back work they never completed. I'm starting to get some in. I want to have all recent tests and papers corrected and out of the way by the time the finals get here, which right now is only three days away.

Apparently there is some sort of teacher checklist to be completed before we are actually done for the year. I better find it and do it. Of course, I should've been aware of it nine months ago, but better late than never.

I had a good discussion with a colleague today about whether or not to teach values and/or morals in a Senior Contemporary Issues class. It's a touchy issue, but that doesn't mean I'll shy away from it.

The halls are a bit quieter now that the Seniors are gone. I'd say about 20 percent fewer people, and about 40 percent quieter. I wouldn't have guessed it would be that much of a different feeling with them gone. Frankly, it's much better.

Tuesday. I came in early to get papers corrected and entered in the gradebook and computer so I could get them back to students. I didn't completely finish, and will wrestle with that in bits and pieces during the next couple days.

Later in the day I caught a few moments and made up the history exam for later this week. It feels good to have it done and copied and ready to go a couple days ahead of time. I suppose it'd be better to have it done weeks ahead of time, but I haven't known what I wanted to put on my tests until after the last day before the test. You never know what interesting stuff will come up that should be integrated into the lesson. For example, this morning's paper had an article on "Nannygate," referring to the Clinton Administration appointees who failed to pay taxes properly, and were disqualified from consideration for positions they had been nominated for. We are just ending our Watergate unit, and the article tied in perfectly.

I'm feeling a bit down. I wonder if it's hitting me, that this year is really about one day from ending, and my time with these kids will be over. I've spent more time with them than their parents have, with only a few exceptions. I'm wondering if I'll miss them and how I could've done a better job. Maybe selfishly I want to look better in their eyes. To be impressive, and maybe — probably — I wasn't. I guess anyone can look back on anything with those types of thoughts.

I didn't have a full period of Law planned, and it ended about ten minutes early. Right when I finished my prepared stuff, the class went completely silent. I was thinking, if ever there was a good opportunity to go on to something else, that was it. But lack of preparation allowed a good chance to get by.

I'm starting to figure how I'll word my class rules for next year. It will be much more complete and much more explicit regarding expectations and requirements. I will run my classes basically like A.P. classes, except without all the work. We'll see.

Wednesday. Today was AIDS day in my history classes. It was a fairly significant day, because we talked about sex, morals, behaviors, societal problems and the like.

As has been happening lately, I've been the recipient of fortunate timing. Today's newspaper had a headline about AIDS being the leading killer in many major cities. I posted that headline and article on the podium so it was in front of everyone as we discussed the issue. We talked about the fallacy of "safe sex," the change in morals since the days of the students' grandparents, and what we could or should do about behaviors in society. The media came up as the big culprit, but we all acknowledged that lack of individual accountability and responsibility is the problem. We also dealt with some scientific aspects of the virus, which I am woefully ignorant about. Of the three classes, two went fine, one went too fast and unorganized. I can see that next year I need to allocate more time for it.

I got all my final tests together for Thursday and Friday. Today was the last day of actual classes. I'm only giving one hour tests, which is a mistake, because the test days are divided into three two-hour testing periods, and many kids get the one-hour test done in under 45 minutes. Next year, I will have semester, or possibly year-end, cumulative finals. To fill the extra hour, I went to the video store and got a comedy video. I'll review it later tonight to make sure it's okay. I caught myself thinking, as I was trying to pick something they'd like, that they wouldn't appreciate any type of movie classic, even an old mystery or musical. Too bad, but they are really affected by the modern extremism entertainment culture.

I received a nice compliment from an administrator today, and it felt good, though I know my faults. I'm mentally getting ready for next year regarding changes I'll make. If I were smart, I'd type out my class rules for next year now, while the specifics and the reasons for the specifics are still in my brain.

Thursday. Today was the first day of tests. Some teachers, me included, have scrambled to have some activity or video available for when after the kids are done with their tests. A veteran teacher I respect designs his test to last the whole two hours. It's a good test and keeps the kids busy. We have been given the word to keep the kids in the classroom, so that's what we're trying to achieve.

One thing I did not anticipate was how boring, almost lonely, today would be. I'm just there while the kids are taking the tests. Then I correct them. Not much interaction.

After one test, I showed the "Bronx Video." At first the class thought it was, well, boring is too nice of a word. But fairly early on in the video, when students started appearing on camera, interest picked up dramatically. One student thought it was a bit weak, but this was one who declined to be part of it. I pointed out, with some gentleness but maybe a bit too directly, if one chooses not to be part of a project, they've lost the right to complain about it. The main complaint the kids had was that the video made them look like hicks. It didn't, but, even across country to kids they'll never see, image is everything.

I corrected most of the papers from today, but not all. I'll be in early tomorrow to get more done, and during the first test section tomorrow,

I'll finish grading today's papers. I noticed that the new computer in my room does not accept my grade disk, and I won't pretend to know why. I'll just use my home computer to finish out the year and worry about this computer later.

Today, after weeks of getting dozens of rejection letters from publishers regarding this journal, I received a positive response. They are interested in publishing, but want more information. As I told my wife, that's like being on first base, but my no means home.

I still need to clean out my room. I haven't had the heart to take down all the posters and such that the kids made during the year. I'll do it after the last class is gone the last day, which will be next Monday. Also, I need to go through four filing cabinets and clear out all the old stuff. I will be starting out much more efficiently next year.

Friday. More of the same from yesterday. The kids are still focused during the tests. I have arranged the tests in History to include more matching and less essay than usual. The bad, but true, reason for that is that they will be easier to grade, and there is a time crunch here. The grades are due Monday, and I have a personal commitment this weekend, so I better get as much of this done as I can while in class. I graded the matching part as it came in, so I got all of that done. I didn't get any of the essays graded, nor any of the teen law tests. That will have to wait until Saturday and Sunday evenings.

The day went slowly, and I missed "teaching." However, again it's a relief when the kids are working on the test, and they actually finish it and turn it in, like it makes sense. Some teachers gave their "final" several days ago when the Seniors were still in class, and avoided the last minute, after-hours, correcting and grading rush. Their position, which seems reasonable, would be that they're getting paid for what they can do during the school hours.

Many of the kids said they won't be back Monday. It's a half-day make-up from a snow day. It will be basically meaningless, but a chance to chat for a bit and say goodbye for the summer. Also, there will be more administrative stuff to do, like making sure their books and registrations are checked in. I am debating whether or how to tell them about this book. Now that I've got a favorable response from a publisher, it will be more fun, more real, to talk about.

178

✒ 39th Week: Jun. 21st

I had a student read the one publisher's letter indicating interest in this project. It was a fun moment, complete with polite applause. I told them they were the stars of the show, and they are.

Monday, June 21st. I am home after the last day of the school year. Classes today were each 20 minutes long. Or short. Mainly, all we did was check in some books and chat about summer plans.

The last day of school has a lot of possibilities. It could be a little emotional. I guess that's a reaction you feel regarding some of the kids, and maybe more so after the first year, which is an emotional roller coaster in any event. I'm glad it's over, but I regret not being a better teacher. I reminded the kids that we just spent about five hours a week together — more time than many, probably most of them, spend with their parents. I will wonder how they progress. Fortunately, I'll see them around next year because most of them are Juniors.

Last night I was grading papers until a bit past midnight and getting my computer sheets in order, so they could be posted this morning with final grades. I don't have to do that. I could simply tell the kids that I haven't got all the grades done yet and that they'll have to wait until they get their report cards to get the grades. There are two problems with that: First, it wouldn't be honest, and second, the whole reason we're here is for the kids, and if any of them want to talk to me about their grade, they ought to be able to do so. In fact, only a few even checked them, and no one had any changes or challenges.

I also told my three all-year (history) classes about this journal. I handed out three rejection letters from publishers and had some students read them. Then they knew what was up. I had a student read the one publisher's letter indicating interest in this project. It was a fun moment, complete with polite applause. I told them they were the stars of the show, and they are.

After the kids were gone, I completed my grade sheets and turned them in. There is a check-out procedure in the back of the teacher's manual which I had not looked at until recently. It lists the things each teacher must do or turn in before being officially "done" for the year. The duties included getting all the grade sheets in, turning in your gradebook, and turning in your textbook return list which shows which students still owe books. There is also a section which allows you to present comments on how to improve the school.

I weighed the item regarding how we could improve the school. It's not a subject that can be dealt with in a cursory manner, so I didn't address that optional question.

I will keep my gradebook neater and more organized next year, knowing that it goes into some sort of permanent vault or something. I made copies of it, so if a student or parent has a question about a grade, I can show why I did what I did. Regarding the grades, I found myself nudging a few students up half a grade if they were on the line and if they participated in class.

Also, just like the students, I needed to get cleared from the library. I owe $3.50 for one lost one magazine.

I started going through the drawers to throw out old stuff. The tricky part is how to define "old stuff." Around home, our motto is, "When in doubt, throw it out." I'm not quite that bold here, where I may need that odd something next fall.

Soon I will make a Class Rules or Student Expectations sheet for next year. It will be much more detailed and direct and will deal plainly with curriculum and conduct. I will make sure I have it available for easy reference, so there is no confusion. This will enable me to take consistent, remedial action when necessary.

A veteran mentioned that the janitors will do a locker clean-out in about three days, a great time to get supplies for next year and to get back some of the stuff we loaned out during the year. Kind of what goes around comes around.

Even though it was rainy, today I wore baggy swim trunks to school. I figured if they make us come to school after June 20th, the dress code is out the window. The principal agreed, though one of the vice-principals, after looking at my not-so-tan legs, joked it wasn't so much a bold statement of summertime as it was a new version of bad taste.

After the last class, a few teachers went to a local pizza place. It was packed with high school kids. A few of them, in response to the discussion about this journal, yelled out across the room, "Mr. Gish, may I go to the bathroom?"

Yes, you may. And thank you very much.

A Look Back — A Look Ahead

It is April of my second year. The reason for the delay in getting this done has to do with the mechanics of publishing and editing, in addition to having time for normal life with my wife and four kids, working on our mini-farm, and, oh yes, being a second-year teacher. Now, of course, I'm an expert. I can look back at my first year and see the mistakes, problems, opportunities, successes and failures from a new perspective.

In the last few months I have spent some time going over the journal and getting it ready for publication. Going through that process brought the year vividly — sometimes painfully — back to mind. I think it is worthwhile to reflect on what happened from my new perspective. Perhaps "reflect" isn't the right word. More like mop up.

There is a difference between being a first-year teacher and being a teacher. After experiencing how things progress, what type of action gets what type of response, I feel that now, late in my second year, I am ready to teach, not just survive. In one way I wish this journal could be about the second year. I am a better teacher than I was last year. I use time more efficiently, get more out of the kids, allow less misbehavior, and generally have tightened things up. As a consequence, everything is better.

At the risk of being too mundane, I want to discuss some specific changes I've made, dealing both with my conceptions and philosophy of education generally and with specific in-class methods. I say "some" because there's no way I could possibly touch on everything I've learned. Anyway, in no real order, here goes:

Class rules need to be detailed and enforceable. I assumed a higher level of maturity and cooperation than I got from a few of the kids. Most of the kids don't need rules, so in addressing this issue it is helpful to remember who they're for and to be fairly strict and certain. One good example of realizing you have to be willing to make a rule and follow it happened just a couple days ago. A student was being sassy, so I called him up to my desk to discuss the situation. I asked him what he thought should be done. His response was direct and accurate: "Well, Mr. Gish, I don't know. I'm not getting paid to make the decisions around here." He's right. I am. I will.

This brings up a larger issue — whether there should be class-by-class rules or more of a top-down approach, where the principal has one set of rules that apply to all classes. That would promote consistency, and therefore to some degree, enforceability. My principal hasn't done it that way, and I appreciate his reasoning: We are all professionals and don't like someone telling us what to do all the time. We are under many constraints already, so giving the teacher some freedom to pursue the job in his or her own way is an understandable goal. Even for my second year, I didn't devise a very detailed set of rules, but I acted as if I did, and the kids caught on. Next year, I will follow my own advice and have a more comprehensive set of written rules and expectations.

I no longer allow test re-takes. I still see the validity in them, but I also see the abuse. This year, I made sure my students knew up front that no re-takes were allowed, and I believed this helped some kids focus from the outset. With others, it didn't help, but neither would re-takes help. Last year I "carried" some kids too much. This year, I have some who will probably flunk. I'll go out of my way to help and encourage them, but if they continuously decide not to do the work, I'll continuously decide to give them an F. In short, more accountability.

Early on in the journal I made a reference to some kids missing basic questions, such as, "What is this chapter about?" That didn't happen this year. I am more aware of how well each kid is tuned in, and I have not hesitated to approach, help, or confront a student to get more involved. I have been much more aggressive in dealing with how the kids are doing, not worrying about how I am doing.

I made some references to the effect that I shouldn't blame the kid if he's not focused on me if I don't have a great lesson for the day. For the most part, that's wrong. Letterman probably has a dozen writers and only one show a day. A teacher is on his own with five classes per day. It is the student's responsibility to focus on his or her classwork regardless of whether or not it is exciting. In real life, we cannot limit our performance to those things which we think are exciting and innovative every day. To a slight degree, however, I sympathize with the kids if things become too routine, so I am still on the search for new ideas.

I am using time much more efficiently. In reviewing the journal, it seemed I allowed a "work day," which was really a play day, every so often. Some kids used that time productively, while others did not. I didn't do that this year, though the kids do request that type of thing. On that score, I'm also taking my classes closer to the end of the period with the work we are doing. In my history and law classes, I remember last year, if there was a logical break in the material, I often would stop with about ten minutes to go in class. This year, with a few exceptions, I'll start a new topic or continue to plow through until about two minutes to go. The students and I are better off for it, and it is one stab at avoiding the conspiracy of the least.

That brings up another topic — planning. I am still a near-rookie at this, but I'm getting much better, which simply means being more disciplined and spending more time doing it. However well you can do something with moderate planning, there are benefits to even more planning: You do a better job, which benefits your students; you have the satisfaction of a job well done; you're more relaxed because you are prepared; and class time is just plain easier.

I've continued searching for alternative ways of getting information to the kids, including inviting guest speakers and using videos and other media. The journal makes it appear that I ran many videos, especially in the last few weeks. I guess the journal doesn't lie, but it didn't seem like there were that many days used for that. In any event, there are some good videos, but it takes planning and screening time to find what you want to show and to arrange showing it at the right time in your teaching sequence. Videos can be valuable teaching tools if there is good preparation and follow-up, and a tie-in to the subject at hand. I guess that could be said for any method of dispensing information. I am also using the daily paper more than last year, mostly because I am teaching contemporary issues classes. While checking the paper everyday for those classes, I come across items relating to my law and history classes.

I view my job more from the parents' point of view than I did last year. After dealing with several parents, and getting good feedback about their expectations and my performance, I am reminded that parents not only hope, but expect that I'll challenge their child to learn and do their best. If that creates a problem with the child, that's okay, even expected, because no one likes to be pushed.

I was told a few things after the year was over that relieved some of my anxieties about my performance and my perceptions of school.

My math class was not expected to be a model class. In it were students who were not high in the discipline category, so just getting through the class in one piece was something of a victory.

Regarding that class, another lesson we all know was reinforced: Earlier this year, I saw the student who openly talked about her sex life in town, looking quite pregnant and depressed. I guess actions do have consequences. As her teacher, I think back to whether I could've offered her some advice or somehow had a credible message that might have influenced her. I guess inaction has consequences, too.

Throughout the journal, I talked about the self-centeredness I experienced the first year. That was a valid point then, but I find those concerns or insecurities are fading fast. I now focus not so much on how I am being perceived, but on how to do the best job, however that is defined. Certainly, I am somewhat concerned with how the kids perceive me because credibility is necessary to effective communication. But don't get bogged down with self, or with trying to give favors to the kids to appease them. I am much tougher this year. A pop run is now unheard of. I freely move a chatty student without regard to his, her, or the class's reaction to the move. I can't believe how I agonized over that last year.

By early October in my second year, most of my classes had developed a sense of camaraderie not achieved last year until about April. I was more relaxed, and we got off to a better start. In History, I'm skipping much of what I would call minutia. I have tried, with some success, to limit my time to major issues, covered chronologically. We'll benefit from that this spring, with more time for more recent history and current events.

In the Absolutely Mundane But Practical department, I rearranged the desks. They're in rows, angled toward the center of the room. This allows space between the students, which cuts down on chit-chat (not to mention that the janitor likes it because he can get his broom through there). The reason for the angle toward the center is that I dislike traditional rows for a discussion class. This compromise seems to work, although I notice most veterans use traditional rows.

There are huge issues regarding teaching and public schooling, which I said this journal will not be about, but since this relates to what I think will be part of the teacher's role in the future, I'd like to comment on it.

Some blame society's problems on schools and teachers, which is like blaming the heat for the fire. Our schools reflect what is going on in society, much of which is getting worse. Our society is looking in the mirror to see where it can improve. One part of society is our schools, so they, too, are being examined.

We are asking why we have schools in the first place, and wondering if our goals are being accomplished. We need to remember that schools as we know them are merely a blip on the screen of our existence. Certainly we need to provide opportunities for learning, but we shouldn't automatically endorse the herd method that we see in our system of "cells and bells."

There are some claims the system is "dumbing down" all the kids. Where that does exist stems from the desire of our system to carry everyone, sometimes even against their own wishes. I have seen that I need to be plain tougher — to create and expect more accountability.

We now have a system that passes everyone regardless of the limited understanding of some. As someone pointed out, time is the constant, and achievement is the variable. Ask a child how old he is, and the answer may be something like, "Fifth grade." We need to change it so achievement is a constant, to some level of actual understanding or mastery, and time is a variable.

Our system puts students in the classroom who have no business being there, either because of ability or choice. We need to move toward the European model of schools, wherein kids make a decision (not irreversible) at about eighth or ninth grade (or when they achieve a certificate of mastery in the basics) regarding what type, if any, of high school they'd like to attend. Some call that "tracking," and some don't like the word. The label doesn't matter — the result is what we need to focus on.

Allowing kids to pursue their interests would limit the population at either the academic or trade or art schools to those who want to be there, and they would be able to get a better education, less encumbered with the discipline and performance problems caused by those who shouldn't be there. Hand-in-hand with that, we must elevate our perception of those who choose not to go to the academic schools. Let's recognize that a person with a trade is as worthy as, and often financially better off than, a college graduate with nothing but a diploma. Vocational or trade programs need community support, with apprenticeships aggressively supported by schools and the community.

This is not meant to be a treatise on how to solve societal problems, but leaving that portion out of a discussion of what schools ought to look like or offer, or whether they should exist at all, makes for an incomplete analysis. Before any form of school is successful, it must be recognized that *family* is the foundation on which all of what the student does is built. Only then will there be the necessary discipline, accountability, and other qualities developed so that the education available at school is nurtured, respected, and applied in some meaningful way.

There is no satisfactory way to finish this work. I learned a ton my first year, and am better my second year. I'll be better next year, and the learning curve will not be so steep. But in this profession, it will never be flat.

I think my experience is typical of the new teacher, and I hope this trip has been worth it.

Copies of
MR. GISH, MAY I GO TO THE BATHROOM?
may be ordered from:

Deer Park Publications
2445 Deer Park Road
Port Angeles, WA 98362
(206) 457-7391

Name: _____

Address: _____

City, State, ZIP: _____

Number of copies @ $9.95 each: _____

Amount: $ _____

(WA residents only) 8.2% sales tax: _____

(All orders) $1.50 postage/handling per copy: _____

TOTAL: $ _____

Please enclose check or money order, payable to:
Deer Park Publications.